Kay Kuzma, Ed.D.

Foreword by Elden M. Chalmers, Ph.D.

REVIEW AND HERALD® PUBLISHING ASSOCIATION
HAGERSTOWN, MD 21740

This book was
Edited by Raymond H. Woolsey
Interior design by Willie S. Duke
Cover design by Ron J. Pride
Cover photo by Zigy Kaluzny ©Tony Stone Images
Typeset: 10/11 Utopia

01 00 99 98 97 5 4 3 2 1

R&H Cataloging Services
Kuzma, Kay Judeen Humpal, 1941-
Easy obedience: teaching children self-discipline with love.

1. Obedience. 2. Self-control. 3. Child rearing.
I. Title.

179.9

ISBN 0-8280-1084-6

Dedication

To my son, Kevin, who inspired this book and unselfishly gave me permission to use personal illustrations so that other families could discover the joy of easy obedience.

To my grandson, Tristan James Ivkov, who is just beginning his journey toward easy obedience.

And to the other precious Kevins and Tristans of the world, that through the love and understanding of you, the reader, they may learn to know their loving Father in heaven and be led to respond willingly to His call "Come unto Me."

Acknowledgments

To June Patterson, the director of the early childhood unit at the University Elementary School at UCLA, who "tutored" me through my first year of teaching, where I encountered my first challenging child: Brad!

To my husband, Jan, who was the codirector of the experimental journey we took together in parenting our three children.

To our three children, Kimberly Ivkov, Karlene St. Clair, and Kevin Kuzma, who were my greatest teachers.

And to those who read and critiqued the manuscript for this book, for their valuable insight and enthusiasm for easy obedience: Elden and Esther Chalmers, Allan and Jill Kennedy, and Greg and Diane Pratt.

Contents

Foreword

Never before has teaching children to obey been made so easy and so much fun as in this book! With a penetrating insight that sees through the many masks that both children and parents wear, Kay Kuzma gets to the roots of the wide variety of parenting problems—the drive for attention, for power, or for revenge, to name just a few. With fascinating and easy-to-follow examples, Kay shows how to love children into willing and joyful obedience. Frustrated, exasperated, and exhausted parents will discover their own God-given sense of humor as they fascinate their children into obedience.

If you know you were born to be a dictator, you'll enjoy learning how to be a good one in Kay's sketch of the "benevolent dictator."

If you are forever plunging headlong into confrontations with your children, you'll love her instructions on how to prepare for them.

If you are tired of always saying no to your children, you'll discover how you will never have to say no again—and both you and your children will love it!

If you know you have been making too many "impossible" rules for your children, you'll be glad for the section on setting obeyable limits.

If you have found that your punishments don't work, you'll find new ones that really do.

If you've wondered about "sparing the rod and spoiling the child," you'll wonder no longer after her chapter on shock therapy.

In her book Kay Kuzma tackles some of the most challenging real-life examples of defiance, rebellion, stubbornness, indifference, rejection, loneliness, depression, excitability, and distractibility, and provides you with unique, creative real-life examples of how to deal with them.

This hard-to-put-down book is a must for all parents, and for family life professionals who are looking for creative and practical solutions for their clients. Easy to read, yet scientifically and biblically sound, it provides amazingly comprehensive coverage of effective parenting issues.

—*Elden M. Chalmers, Ph.D.*

Introduction

Benjamin Franklin once said, "Let thy child's first lesson be obedience, and the second will be what thou wilt." That's sage advice. But is obedience ever really *easy?* Some might argue that it's impossible! But I disagree.

Parenting will always have its challenges, but with the foundation of understanding love, and the willingness to meet your children's basic needs, you can apply the techniques found in this book and experience the pleasure of rearing a child who is generally willing to obey.

This doesn't mean the child is faultless. We all make mistakes. But children who know without a shadow of a doubt that they are loved irrationally—not for any reason except that they exist—seldom if ever have a hidden agenda of rebellion. And rebellion is the primary element that makes it so tough to get children to obey.

This is really a book about the importance of *self-discipline.* Because trying to discipline others is always difficult. In fact, having to "make" another person obey is probably the toughest job in the world, especially if there is little or no respect. Unfortunately, far too many parents think making children obey is what parenting is all about. I'd like to change that concept. Instead, our job should be to encourage children to become self-disciplined.

The Amplified Bible puts it this way: "Train up a child in the way he should go [and in keeping with his individual gift or bent], and when he is old he will not depart from it" (Prov. 22:6). Easy obedience is based on this biblical concept to train up a child in the way *he* or *she* should go. Each child has unique needs and desires, as well as a unique personality. When you respect a child for the unique person he or she is, and, considering the age factor, train within those parameters, the lesson of obedience can be more easily taught. Our job as parents is to set up an environment that is conducive to growth. Our actions and words, our admonitions and limits, should provide a warm, secure atmosphere in which children will find it easy to respect and obey the wishes of those in authority.

To discipline really means to teach. In fact, the same techniques that are successful in the classroom can revolutionize your home. So, based on the foundation of educational theory and practice, coupled with the practical experience my husband, Jan, and I have had of rearing three children who are now loving and responsible adults, I offer you a method of discipline that has stood the test of time. Many have come to me now that their children are grown and said, "I raised my kids with the Kuzma method, and I wish you could meet them. They are such nice people to be around!"

I hope that in the years to come you will be one of those parents!

—Kay Kuzma
Cleveland, Tennessee

Chapter 1

Lessons I've Learned From Children

Children have more need of models than of critics.—Joseph Joubert.

Many parents have paraphrased the seventeenth-century English poet John Wilmot, Earl of Rochester, when he said, "Before I got married I had six theories about bringing up children; now I have six children and no theories."

We chuckle at those words—those of us with children—because we too have stumbled into the parenting job with some definite ideas of "how to," only to have them shattered by our children. But in the end, it is not as if we were left void. We have learned something. We may have not survived with our original theories intact, but what we have learned is valid—even if the lesson is merely the fact that there are many ways to raise children.

And so it has been with me. I may not have survived parenthood with all my preparenting theories intact, but children have taught me some valuable lessons—four with which I begin this book. And if you will use the four crucial lessons I've learned to form your theories of child rearing, I will guarantee that you can significantly increase your chances of achieving the goal of easy obedience with your children.

Lesson 1: Respect is the basis of easy obedience.

I had what some may consider a parenting advantage. I taught children before I had my own. That was valuable experience. And it was at the University Elementary School at UCLA, where I was one of five teachers in an experimental multiage team-teaching program of 60 preschool children, that I learned my first lesson about obedience. The teacher? The most challenging 4-year-old I have ever encountered.

I'll call him Brad. He literally gave me nightmares. Brad was uncontrollable and defiant, acting as if he were on a secret mission to destroy my fledgling teaching career. His method of attack? Disobedience! Regardless of what I said or did, he would throw things when he got angry and then would run away so I couldn't catch him—making me look foolish and incompetent. I tried everything I knew to stop this behavior: I watched his rising frustration level and moved in close to forestall an explosion; I imposed consequences; I talked to his mother; I isolated him; I tried not to make him angry; and I finally gave up! Nothing worked.

It was then that my team of teachers made a valuable observation. Brad didn't act this way with them. Obviously, he was testing my authority—and I was flunking. Since he could get away with doing the opposite of whatever I said, he didn't respect me.

Putting our heads together, our team came up with a plan. The next time Brad started to throw something, I was to say firmly, "Put it down." If he threw the object and started to run, I'd command, "Come to me." If he kept running, I was to yell, "*Stop!*" to make sure Brad heard me and at the same time alert my team to the fact that I was about to leave my post of duty so they could cover for me. Then I was to run however far was necessary, catch the child, and take however long it would take to make sure he knew I meant what I said.

A few days later something happened that made Brad angry, and he picked up a block. I warned, "Brad, put the block on the floor." He took one look at me and threw the block, missing a child's face by a fraction of an inch, and turned to run. When I yelled, "Brad, *stop!*" he looked up at me as if to say "I dare you" and ran out the door and into the play yard. I must have surprised the socks off Brad by dashing off after him. He ran toward the little creek that separated our yard from the other classrooms. I finally caught up with him in the upper-grade yard, clamped a firm grip around his arms and waist, and sat down on a rock with a squirming, screaming, cursing mass of rebellion in my lap.

I had only one goal now—to teach this child to respect my authority. I was tempted to get angry. I was tempted to shake some sense into him. I was tempted to squeeze until it hurt. I was tempted to call him names. But I didn't. How could I expect him to respect me if I didn't treat him with respect? So I merely held him firmly and softly repeated, "Brad, you're special. You're a special boy." After what seemed like an eternity his body relaxed. Finally he asked, "What are you gonna do with me?"

"What do you think I should do?" I asked.

He shrugged his shoulders and said, "Beat me."

"But I don't believe in hitting children."

"You don't?" He seemed surprised.

I loosened my grip. "No, especially someone special. But you have to learn to obey me. You have to learn that I mean what I say. You can't throw things at school. Do you understand? When you get angry you can talk—*you can throw words,* not things. And if you start to run and I say *stop,* what are you supposed to do?"

"Stop!"

"And if you disobey me, what will happen?"

"You'll catch me!"

"That's right. And next time there will be a terrible consequence. Do you understand?"

"What are you going to do?"

"The kids at this school obey their teachers. If you can't obey, you won't be able to come to this school. Then your parents will be angry, and all your classmates will miss you, and you won't be able to play with the toys at school. You wouldn't want that to happen, would you?"

"No."

"Then does that mean you're going to obey me?"

"Yes!"

"Great! That's my special kid," I said as I gave him a hug and we walked back to the class together.

Brad never again tested my authority. I had passed. And the lesson for me has lasted three decades: mutual respect is a prerequisite for easy obedience. It's true that you can get obedience without it, but the obedience will be based on the fear of punishment. Take away the fear of punishment, and obedience crumbles like a clay pot before it's fired. How much better to have obedience based on mutual respect—and fired with love!

Lesson 2: Example is a powerful teacher.

Kim, our firstborn, taught me a powerful lesson when she was just a year old. I had an appointment to have her picture taken and had spent about an hour getting her bathed and dressed in a frilly mint-green outfit with matching panties and bonnet; white, lacy socks; and black patent leather shoes.

I left her sitting on a blanket in the backyard for a moment and ran back into the house to put a comb through my hair and grab my purse. It never dawned on me that Kim would leave the blanket, but she did. She crawled across the cement patio, scuffing her brand-new patent shoes (she was not yet walking). And then she discovered the dish half full of mushy dog food. She thrust her hands into it and squeezed it through her fingers. She tasted it. When I finally spotted her, Kim was beginning to smear dog food on the patio door. Yuck! What a mess! Dog food everywhere!

One look and I forgot all my previous child rearing resolutions about not getting angry and spanking. I screamed, "Kimi, what have you done?" Then I picked her up like no 12-month-old should be picked up, slung her over my shoulder, and went spank, spank, spank on her heavily diapered bottom.

Instead of crying, since it really hadn't hurt her, Kim merely reared back in my arms, lifted her little hand, and slapped me across the face.

Two important things that I had learned in graduate school suddenly flashed into my mind: first, children are not for hitting; and second, you should never allow a child to treat you with disrespect. I had just violated the first rule, and Kim, the second. The problem was, I knew better; Kim didn't. She was merely copying my behavior. I had hit her, so she hit me!

I then thought of a cartoon wherein a father was saying, as he spanked his child, "Hopefully this will teach you that you are never to hit anyone smaller than yourself!"

Obviously, the worst possible way to teach children not to hit is to hit them. Children are imitators, especially during the first three or four years, and you must be extremely careful what you do and say in their presence if you don't want it repeated!

I didn't hit Kim again, for if I had she probably would have hit me back again, until such a time as I would hit her so hard that she would finally have learned that children are not supposed to hit adults even though adults hit them. I didn't want to do that. I was the one who had erred. Not only had I hit her, but I shouldn't have left her alone. She didn't know she shouldn't play with the dog food!

Right then I realized that telling parents they should never discipline in anger was easier said than done. I was shocked that such a little thing had made me so angry that I literally forgot all my training in child development and all the resolutions I'd made about the way I wanted to discipline my children. I also realized that if parents really want to treat their children with respect, it is vitally essential for them to control their anger. Hitting a 12-month-old is a blatant act of disrespect—and anger was the root cause. There were far better ways to teach the lesson not to touch the dog food.

Kim's reaction to my hitting her and the lesson I learned from it will be forever etched in my memory, and I hope you'll remember it too: Treat your children the way you want your children to treat you—and others—because they will end up imitating you. Children are like wet cement. The younger they are, the easier it is to make an impression on them, an impression that may last a lifetime. Example is a powerful teacher.

Lesson 3: Encouragement makes it easier to obey.

Child psychiatrist Rudolf Dreikurs once said, "Encouragement is more important than any other aspect of child rearing. It is so important that the lack of it can be considered the basic cause for misbehavior. A misbehaving child is a discouraged child. Each child needs continuous encouragement, just as a plant needs water. He cannot grow and develop and gain a sense of belonging without encouragement."

For me, it was just a theoretical statement until one day when Kari, our second, was 3 years old. She was an intense child—intensely happy and intensely sad, intensely good and intensely bad! For a number of weeks we noticed the sunshine and laughter had disappeared from our little Kari, and her negative attitude was difficult to live with. She always seemed to be doing things that forced us to correct her. "Kari, stop that." "Kari, watch out." "Kari, you need to listen."

Then early one morning Jan read Dreikurs' statement. "Could it be," he asked, "that the negative, critical way we have been treating Kari is causing more misbehavior instead of less?"

To test the theory, we decided that no matter what Kari did, we would find something positive to say. We would support and encourage her, and see if it made a difference.

When Jan woke her that morning, he whispered in her ear what a special child she was. He asked her if she would like some help getting dressed so she could help him feed the horses. (Kari loved horses!) For the next half hour he gave her extra attention and praise. By the time Kari and her dad got back from the barn, Kari was a different child. "Daddy, I love you." "Daddy, may I sit by you?" "Daddy, can I help you make the toast?"

Then after breakfast, when Kari happily ran into the bathroom to brush her teeth—a task she had refused to do before—Jan and I looked at each other and smiled that "ah-ha" smile, acknowledging that once again Dreikurs was right. We continued our experiment for a week, and never again did we see the negative behavior to the extent we had seen it before we started encouraging. The little grouch had disappeared, and we were once more blessed with the warmth of her laughter.

What made the difference? Our criticism had discouraged her, and we ended up with a misbehaving child. Our encouragement and acceptance gave her a new sense of hope and enough ego strength to discipline herself into more appropriate behavior.

I can't tell you how much that one experiment did to change the basic trend of our parenting. It's easy for parents to fall into the rut of criticizing a child for mistakes and constantly correcting misbehavior, thinking that will teach the child appropriate behavior.

But how much better it is to focus on encouraging your child in the hope of preventing the misbehavior in the first place. Children tend to live up to the expectations we have for them. Encouragement says "You can do it!" "You are special!" "I trust you to do your best." Criticism says "You're no good. You're a failure!"

If you want your child to be willing to obey, eager to please you, and generally compliant rather than defiant, start out with a heavy dose of encouragement. I think you'll find, as we did, that encouragement forms the positive environment in which children thrive.

Lesson 4: Teaching obedience can be fun.

Kevin, our third, took all our creative parenting energy we could muster to teach him the obedience lesson. But in the process he taught us something, too: teaching obedience can be fun. Here's how I first learned that lesson.

"Kevin, I need your help," I said one hurried morning. "We have 15 minutes before we have to leave for school, and I can't get everything done by myself."

"But I don't want to help."

"Well, what will it take to change your mind?"

"What will you give me?" responded 9-year-old Kevin, his eyes gleaming with the opportunity to bargain for something special.

Not wanting to be bribed into promising the moon, I told him I'd give him a hug.

"That's not enough," responded Kevin, with visions of sugarplums and dimes dancing before his eyes.

"OK," I said, willing to bargain. "I'll just have to give you something else."

"What?" replied Kevin eagerly.

"For everything you do for me, I'll give you not only a hug but also a kiss!"

This was not what Kevin wanted—or expected. "Not enough," he said again, shaking his head.

Well, enough of that sweet stuff! I thought. *I'll end up bargaining the 15 minutes away.*

"All right," I said, "for everything you do for me I'll give you a hug and a kiss—and a kick in the pants."

"A what?" he asked, startled.

"A kick in the pants," I repeated.

"No," he laughed as he shook his head. "That's still not enough." But I could tell he was less resistant.

"OK, I'll give you something else if you really want it."

"What?" he asked again.

"Well," I hesitated, "I'll give you a hug and a kiss . . . and a kick in the pants . . . and . . . and a nibble on the ear."

He hesitated momentarily, as if he couldn't believe this was coming from his mom, and then shouted, "I'll take it!"

Eager to see if I'd hold to my bargain, he asked, "What do you want me to do?"

"Make your bed," I directed.

He ran to his room, pulled up the covers, positioned his pillow, and smoothed it all out.

"Done," he shouted as he ran to me for his reward. I bent down and kissed him. Then while hugging him tight, I reached around his body with my foot and tapped him on his behind and then tried to nibble his ear.

"Stop," he giggled. "What next?"

"The dirty clothes need to be carried to the laundry room." Off he ran, appearing moments later for a repeat performance.

Wow, did Kevin work! Fifteen minutes of double time, while I was kept busy hugging, kissing, kicking, and nibbling.

Now, I would never suggest that a kick in the pants is the answer for a parent who complains of a child balking when it comes to housework. Nor would I mention hugging, kissing, and nibbling to get a kid to obey. It probably wouldn't work for your child. It probably wouldn't have worked again with Kevin. But we sure had a great time with the game while it lasted—and it certainly was effective in getting Kevin to do what needed to be done.

"That's a bunch of nonsense," you say. "You should tell a child once, and that child had better jolly well do it, or else! Parents shouldn't have to play games to get their children to obey."

Maybe not. But life is a whole lot more pleasant if occasionally you do make a game out of it.

This is just one example of how creativity won the day. Yes, it's true that most parents threaten and shout when a child hesitates to obey. But that only makes the discipline task distasteful to both young and old. If the same lesson of obedience can be taught in a clever, fun-loving way, why not?

I challenge you to be significantly different—to be a creative disciplinarian, and see just how easy obedience can be.

Chapter 2

Goals for Easy Obedience

Parents must decide what quality of family life they will have and then use the necessary discipline to accomplish this. Otherwise life will push the family in diverse directions, and they will be victims rather than disciples.—Gladys Hunt, Honey for a Child's Heart.

Easy obedience uses the preventive approach to discipline. Rather than constantly dealing with disobedience, misbehavior, and rebellion, you need to focus on preventing as many problems as possible. In order to set up a teaching curriculum for easy obedience and the prevention of behavior problems, you must have your outcome variables clearly in mind. What do you want to accomplish? Then you can figure out how to get there!

Do you want unquestioning compliance, with your children jumping to your every whim and fancy—children with no will of their own? I doubt it. You want children who are willing to obey, but ones who can reason from cause to effect, ones who can think for themselves, ones who are good decision-makers, ones who have the strength of character to stand up to peer pressure or say no to abusive relationships.

If this is your ultimate objective, then there are three goals you must have to monitor every parenting decision. Here's what you must ask yourself:

1. Will what I do help my children to become self-disciplined?
2. Will what I do prevent or resolve conflict?
3. Will what I do preserve or build my children's feelings of self-worth?

The importance of self-discipline

I once had a mother come up to me, open her purse, take out a wooden spoon, and wave it. "How long should I have to carry this spoon in my purse?"

"What's it for?" I asked.

"To make my kids obey!" she replied.

I was shocked. "Put it away immediately," I said, "and teach your children self-control."

When children are self-controlled rather than parent-controlled, it frees time for more creative, enjoyable, and happy family interactions. Obedience ceases to be easy the minute you have to force it. It's work to have to stand over your child every minute for fear your little one will step out of line. Overcontrol parenting zaps energy and destroys the feeling of delight and joy that should result in the hours and days and years you spend in an intensive teaching relationship with your children.

Plus, it steals from your children the opportunity to practice decision-making. Good decision-makers aren't born; children learn how to make good decisions by making decisions. Practice makes perfect—or at least it significantly helps.

You must, however, adjust your methods of teaching to the developmental stages of your children. You can't reach the goal of self-discipline by allowing children to practice self-control at a stage in life when they are too young to make good decisions. So you must start your teaching as a "benevolent dictator." You make good decisions for your children and allow them to reap the rewards of those positive decisions. In time your children will begin to model the way you make decisions. When they question the wisdom of your decision, you take time to explain why you made that choice. You constantly teach, and as your children demonstrate their ability to think rationally instead of acting impulsively, you begin to allow them to make age-appropriate decisions. When they make good decisions, you allow them to reap the positive consequences. When they make poor decisions, either the natural consequence or your parent-imposed consequence should be extremely instructive. Most adults will admit that many of the important lessons they learned in life, they learned through trial and error by experiencing consequences.

Even though you begin your parenting career as a benevolent dictator, your goal is to move toward a more democratic form of family government as soon as possible. Just remember, you as a parent are the "president" of your family government. You do have veto power, but the more you can encourage good decision-making, the less you'll have to exercise it—and the easier obedience will be.

The importance of preventing or resolving conflict

You should have seen it coming. It had been a miserable day for 4-year-old Ricky. He had wet the bed again, and you sighed, "Oh, Ricky, not today," because it meant you had to find a slot in your already busy schedule to wash a load of bedding.

Then Scott came over so early from next door that Ricky ate only half his breakfast, even though you protested. An hour later the boys were battling over who was going to drive the new truck over the block road Ricky had worked so hard to make. In the end, the road was kicked all over the room and Scott left yelling, "My daddy's gonna beat you up!"

At that moment you walked in and let Ricky have it. "This room is a sight! You get these blocks picked up immediately." He tried to protest, saying that Scott helped make the mess, but you wouldn't listen, and told him if his room wasn't clean in 30 minutes there would be no afternoon storytime. He didn't make the deadline.

You fixed a lovely casserole for lunch. Ricky took one bite and spit it all over the table, yelling, "Yuck!" You took him down from the table and sent him to his room. He warned you that trouble was ahead when he yelled, "You'll be sorry," but the baby was crying, and (you should have seen it coming!) an hour later Ricky's room looked like a tornado had struck. Everything on his shelves had been thrown to the floor, his wastebasket was upset, and the fresh sheets and blankets were pulled from the bed. *Yes, you should have seen it coming!*

Parents could divert many disasters if they would just anticipate conflicts. Children can take only so much pressure before they explode. If you can see that things aren't going well, forewarn your children. "It looks like you are just about ready to haul off and hit someone. That's probably not such a good idea." Your intervention at critical times can help children gain control of themselves.

Many of the things children do that parents feel must be corrected would never happen if parents were more observant and helped children rechannel their energies before misbehavior occurred. Here are some effective techniques to use when you anticipate difficulties.

1. *Touch control.* Babies who are touched by their parents every 10 or 15 minutes during their awake time are less demanding. Don't talk to them, because that distracts them from their activities; just touch them. Touch is a powerful tool in preventing behavior problems.

If you see frustration building, sometimes a gentle pat, an embrace, or simply placing a hand on your child's shoulder before things explode will serve as a reminder that you are near and will help the child if help is needed. Properly timed, your touch may prevent children from becoming unmanageably aggressive.

2. *Diversion.* When your child becomes frustrated and can't seem to handle the situation even with adult help, diversion to another closely related activity may help. In my early parenting career I found this word of advice in a book called *Child Guidance*: "While they are too young to reason with, divert their minds as best you can." It was very reassuring to know that I didn't have to solve every problem but could simply divert attention to avoid conflict. For example, your child wants a toy another child has. Before it comes to a fight, find a similar toy and make a big deal about how wonderful it is.

3. *Point out reality.* Parents are often surprised at how early it is possible to reason with a child. Even tiny 2-year-olds can understand simple reasoning if you take the time and they're in a receptive mood. Many children become frustrated because they want to do something but

there isn't enough time or space, or the right tools are not available. They become angry and aggressive because they do not understand these limitations. Parents should take the extra time required to explain the reality of the situation and point out what can be done within these limitations. For example: "I don't have apple juice. Let's look in the pantry and see what else we can find." When you are reasoning with a child, it is important that the explanation be short and simple.

A direct appeal for the child's cooperation is often effective with older children. They like to please and be helpful and will usually listen to this direct pointing out of reality. For example, "You need to pay attention to the story because the others want to hear it."

4. *Be involved.* To prevent problems effectively, you have to be an involved parent. Your children ought to believe you have eyes in the back of your head. You don't always have to give away your sources of information. It's not bad to keep a child guessing for a while: "How did Dad know I sneaked out and went to that movie?" "How did Mom find out about that broken window?" You should be involved enough in your children's lives that you can sense when they may have done something wrong, are worried, or are hiding something. One creative mom helped keep her boys from experimenting with alcohol and tobacco by making the policy that each of them had to kiss her good night, no matter how late he got home. Mom could smell alcohol or smoke a block away!

When you see a potential storm brewing, be willing to step in if necessary with a little extra moral support and some creative diversion tactics. You might be able to prevent some major difficulties. Diverting disasters is so much better than having to figure out what kind of creative discipline will teach your child the lesson that misbehavior doesn't pay!

All parents want to establish joyful, loving, high-quality relationships with their children. Obviously, fighting, arguing, demeaning, yelling, ridiculing, swearing, hitting, and threatening are not conducive to such a goal. Such behavior leads only to conflict. After the battle you can kiss and make up, but the bumps and bruises—the physical as well as the psychological ones—are not easily forgotten. It is much better to prevent conflict if possible.

However, in the interest of avoiding conflict in the future, current conflict needs to be dealt with and resolved. Unresolved conflict generally intensifies, resulting in a future explosion. How much better to solve it in the early stages.

Family members should disagree, should stand up for their rights, and should voice their points of view. Family growth is possible only if individuality in thought, as well as behavior, is encouraged. But it is important to settle differences before battle lines are drawn, and before weapons destructive to a child's self-esteem are aimed and fired. Parents should not waste potential high-quality family time in conflict. Neither should they act in such a way as to provoke their children's anger. (Remember the biblical admonition in Colossians 3:21.)

Children's inappropriate behavior ranges from childish irresponsibility (such as forgetting to feed the dog and accidentally spilling the milk) to willful defiance of parental authority. In between these two extremes there is a wide range of "normal" misbehavior by children who persistently challenge the limitations imposed by adults. The task of preventive discipline is to teach a child responsibility and to successfully meet each childhood challenge in a way that will forestall the development of a willfully defiant attitude. A child's willful defiance results in conflict that can destroy parent-child relationships. The following model shows the inappropriate behavior continuum:

CHILDISH IRRESPONSIBILITY

↓

PERSISTENT CHALLENGING OF PARENTAL LIMITATIONS

↓

WILLFUL DEFIANCE OF PARENTAL AUTHORITY

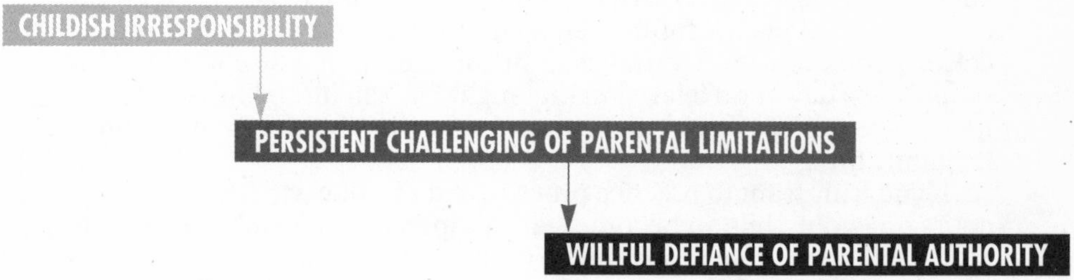

The earlier that intervention (effective discipline) can occur in this inappropriate behavior continuum, the less conflict a family will experience and the easier obedience will be.

In order to avoid unnecessary conflict, a parent must understand the difference between discipline and punishment. Punishment is a penalty imposed upon a child for doing something wrong. Punishment involves the experience of pain, loss, or suffering for a mistake a child has made. Parents usually punish with the intent to hurt a child (physically or emotionally) so that the child will learn that it is painful to do what is wrong and thus choose (or be forced to choose) to do what is right. Parents often punish their children to satisfy their own anger. At other times, parents punish because of a mistaken sense of justice that demands that children must pay a penalty for their "crimes."

Too many people confuse punishment and discipline. They believe that a parent must use punishment to produce a well-disciplined child—a literal "spare the rod and spoil the child" attitude. Actually, when parents punish to eradicate childish irresponsibility and persistent challenging, they may be setting the stage for family conflict. Outward conflict can develop because a child may decide to fight against what he or she considers unjust treatment. Inner conflict may arise because arbitrary punishment can generate feelings of rejection and mistreatment, and children may bottle up intense resentment toward their parents.

Discipline, on the other hand, is a teaching process. It leads to the prevention or the resolution of conflict. Discipline helps children improve themselves. It helps them learn lessons that will make them better people. The primary aims of discipline are to resolve impending conflict and teach children self-discipline.

Punishment is arbitrarily imposed; discipline relates directly to a child's inappropriate behavior. For example, Tim was late getting home from school and had not notified his mother. If she chose to punish him, she might take his bicycle away for two weeks and spank him for his irresponsibility. If, on the other hand, she chose a disciplinary action, she might not allow him to watch his favorite television program that evening so that he could have the time to finish the homework and chores he'd neglected by arriving home late. She might also set up some careful limitations for future behavior: "Unless you call home and receive permission for a variance, you must be home 30 minutes after school each day or no television that night." When discipline is effective, it avoids needless conflict and enhances the possibilities for more quality family time.

If you truly want to practice preventive discipline with the goal of encouraging your child to become self-disciplined and resolve or prevent conflict, then your methods will be based on principles and goals rather than on past experience or present feelings. You must resist the strong tendency to say thoughtlessly, "My parents' methods worked for me, so why shouldn't they work for my children?" Or "I resented the way my parents handled me; I'll never do that to my child."

It is equally harmful to allow feelings to control your actions and assume a laissez-faire attitude or become harsh and punitive in an attempt to win power struggles.

The importance of preserving and building your child's self-worth

Your children will become the persons they believe themselves to be. If they feel worthless, undesirable, and incompetent, these feelings are like a predictive script that they tend to follow in life. But when children feel they are special, when they feel desirable and competent, there is no limit to what they can accomplish. Their potential is great.

The way you discipline will either add to or subtract from a child's feeling of personal value. To monitor the effect of your discipline on your child's self-concept, think about the words you say. Thoughtless words hurt. They can destroy. Before you speak, think how you would feel if the words were directed to you. If they would make you feel worthless and stupid, don't say them to your children. If you do, you're a child abuser.

Before you impulsively say "I would never abuse my child," please read on. Every parent is a potential child abuser. I hate to admit it, but even with all my degrees in child development I have occasionally been abusive. I'll never forget one afternoon when I let my emotions get completely out of control. I had a thousand things to do, and nothing seemed to be going right. The house was in a shambles, and my three preschoolers were running around like a pack of hyenas. The louder they shrieked and hollered, the tighter my nerves wound.

To help me out of my mess, I had asked a teenager to come over and assist me in cleaning the house. Then I turned to my girls. "Kids," I said, "Molly is going to be vacuuming your bedroom soon. Please pick up the clothes that are on the floor." They appeared to have heard me. But like so many parental commands in which parents don't follow through, the words went in one ear and out the other. The clothes remained on the floor. However, this small fact didn't stop Molly from doing her job. She began vacuuming her way around the fallen garments. She had not been told to pick them up, so she left them on the floor. She had not counted on the strong suction of the vacuum, however, and before she knew it she had vacuumed up a beautiful, lace-trimmed nylon nightie.

The motor ground to a stop as the nightgown twisted around the brush and lodged in the vacuum's internal organs. The intense heat melted the nylon, leaving gobs of rock-hard bonding material on the metal parts of the vacuum.

This was the last straw. I couldn't believe the mess. What really upset me was how a teenager could be so careless as not to pick up the children's clothing before vacuuming. Yet I couldn't tell her that. Instead I vented my pent-up frustrations on my girls. I screamed, "Girls, look what you have done now. Why didn't you pick up your clothes? If you had only listened to me this would have never happened."

I began to cry as I started to disassemble the vacuum and realized the magnitude of the mess. "Just look at this mess. Your expensive nightgown is ruined, and this black nylon junk is stuck all over. It will probably cost a fortune to get this vacuum fixed. How could you have been so thoughtless?"

I verbally ripped those kids up one side and down the other, never saying a thing to the teenager who was the immediate cause of the problem. The girls tried to tell me it was not their fault, but I would not listen. Finally, beaten down with verbal abuse, they retreated.

Left alone, scraping off the nylon globs, I began to think about the terrible way I had treated them. I knew better. I had written articles about verbal abuse and how careful we should be not to harm our children with demeaning words. I knew that such careless words could wound a child's sense of self-worth. I had even called such abuse psychological murder. And now I was guilty!

After I took the teenager home, I realized I had to apologize to my children. I called the girls to me, sat them on my lap, and told them how sorry I was for the way I had acted and the terrible things I had said.

Of course they forgave me. But I needed to do one more thing. I needed to make sure this didn't happen again. So I gave my children permission to stop me if I ever verbally abused them again. I told them to say to me, "Mommy, you are out of control, and you told us to stop you."

Most think of child abuse as the harsh, irrational, and violent treatment that leaves children physically injured and scarred for life. Child abuse conjures up in our minds bizarre pictures of children with black eyes and broken bones, first-degree burns from cigarettes or scalding water, whiplash scars across the back and buttocks, or brain damage from having had their heads battered against the wall.

This type of child abuse is a hideous crime. And most parents couldn't imagine ever treating a child in such a way. But there are milder types of child abuse that we're all probably guilty of. The startling fact is that if your child is more than 2 years of age, child abuse has probably occurred in your own home, with you as the abuser and your child as the victim.

Child abuse is more than treatment that results in a physically battered child. It is any treatment that destroys the child's sense of personhood, his or her feelings of self-worth. It is the physical, verbal, or psychological mistreatment of the child. Abusive behavior doesn't have to leave visible scars. It can leave internal scars—the kind that, over time, leave their mark on the child's thinking and personality. These are the scars that destroy self-worth.

If you accept this broad definition of child abuse, then the following behaviors could be considered abusive:

1. Any physical punishment that children feel is unjust or unreasonable, even though it may result in changed behavior.
2. Any impulsive, irrational punishment that is inflicted merely as an appeasement for parental anger.
3. Any treatment of children that makes them feel embarrassed or belittled, especially when it occurs in public.
4. Any words that cut down children's self-respect or diminish the positive feelings they have about themselves.
5. Any behavior that causes children to feel alienated from their family or God.

By now the finger of guilt is probably pointing in your direction. But guilt isn't going to help. What is needed is the firm resolve to discontinue these abusive actions, to discontinue destructive punishment that only builds resentment and rebellion in the heart of your child.

Your actions, too, are important. In fact, your body language may speak louder than your words. Even a look of disappointment can be enough to crush a sensitive child who desperately needs your approval. If you are rigid, rushed, and rude, your children will assume that they aren't worth very much. And children who don't feel very good about themselves are often driven to disruptive behavior in an attempt to get some attention, making it almost impossible for them to obey!

Unreasonable punishment can result in good behavior, but it can destroy a child's self-worth. A child can have many excellent qualities, but if he or she lacks a wholesome sense of self-worth, that person will be at a disadvantage throughout life. When children feel good about themselves, they can choose to become the kind of persons they would like to be. They can choose to avoid or resolve conflict. They can choose to be self-disciplined.

The only way to avoid discipline that is irrational and haphazard is for parents to adopt a disciplinary approach that is based on principles and goals that prevent or resolve conflict. This approach will make it possible to raise a child to have the self-confidence necessary to make wise decisions and be self-disciplined.

Chapter 3

Parenting Styles for Easy Obedience

Our children give us the opportunity to become the parents we always wished we'd had.—Louise Hart.

Were your parents fairly restrictive? Or did you rule the roost? Were they loving and supportive? Or did you at times feel that no one cared? The way your parents treated you programmed your inherited tendencies and has made you what you are. You have the choice to override their work and with God's help reprogram yourself, but once the original programming is in place, change is difficult.

Now you have been given the chance to program another human being. It's an awesome task—one you don't want to botch. As psychologist Louise Hart says: "Our children give us the opportunity to become the parents we always wished we'd had."

How should you parent in order to have the type of children you want? Let's look at the research.

According to one of the earliest studies on parenting styles, published in 1964, the type of parent you are will, to a large extent, determine the characteristics your children will develop. Four parenting styles were examined by Martin and Lois Hoffman in their review of research: the loving-restrictive, which we might call the *authoritative* parent; the loving-permissive, or simply the *permissive* parent; the hostile-restrictive or *authoritarian* parent; and the hostile-permissive or *neglectful* parent.

Types of parenting styles

Let's take a closer look at the characteristics of these four types of parenting styles and what effect they have on children.

Some parents are very loving. They're warm, accepting, and approachable. They enjoy having the children close. They are eager to hug, listen, encourage, and smile. A loving parent is nice to have around.

But on the opposite extreme there are hostile parents. They are cold, rejecting, and distant. "Don't bother me. I've had it! Just leave me alone!" is often the message they give.

There are also restrictive parents and permissive parents. Restrictive ones are those who make a lot of decisions for their children—perhaps too many—and the children are expected to obey consistently.

Permissive parents are those who allow their children to make choices whenever possible—even when they might not be equipped to do so. Those limits that are set are sometimes not consistently enforced.

The midline between restrictive and permissive is best for the children—to have parents who lean toward the more restrictive in early childhood and move toward a more democratic position in the later teens. It's the extremes on this continuum that cause dysfunction. Any time a parent is overly restrictive, making all the rules and demanding exact obedience, or overly permissive, with few or no limits imposed, there is going to be trouble.

Now, let's combine the parental characteristics of loving, rejecting, restrictive, and permissive, and see what type of behavior children are likely to develop.

If you are the loving and restrictive parent—which we sometimes term the *authoritative* parent—you will probably have children who are more submissive and compliant than if you were more permissive. Because of your strong leadership, your children may also be more dependent and not as friendly or creative—but they score high when it comes to being neat, polite, and obedient.

If you are a *permissive* parent who is loving, your children will tend to be socially outgoing, independent, creative, and successfully aggressive—that means aggressive enough to get good grades in school or to get a good job.

In numerous studies the fact is confirmed that parents who are loving have the best chance of their children growing into healthy, productive, secure adults. But parents get into trouble when their children see them as hostile and rejecting.

If children don't feel loved, if their parents are restrictive, *authoritarian* parents, the children often become overly compliant, not able to make their own decisions. They're unsure of themselves, extremely shy with peers, and often develop mental health problems. Children with hostile/rejecting parents are likely to need professional help to overcome the psychological scars they have suffered growing up in dysfunctional homes.

On the other extreme, if parents are hostile and permissive, children tend to be noncompliant and highly aggressive, perhaps even to the extent of becoming delinquents. This type of parent is called a *neglectful* one.

Love is the key factor to raising children who are able to function well in society. If parents are loving, regardless of whether they are more restrictive or permissive, the children will probably do well. It's when parents are hostile and rejecting that children develop antisocial behavior.

It seems pretty clear from these research findings that you have a definite effect on your child's behavior. Of course, you already knew that. But it's especially your love that makes the crucial difference! You want as much love in your relationship with your children as possible, and you will want to avoid any behavior that might be interpreted as hostile or rejecting.

The old tale that a spoiled child was loved too much is just that—an old tale. Too much love doesn't spoil a child—too little discipline (teaching) does! It's impossible to give a child too much of the right kind of love. Children thrive on love that is caring, respecting, accepting, forgiving, and trusting. In fact, the more of this type of love you can give, the better. Love acts like a cushion. The thinner it is, the more parental errors will bump and bruise a child emotionally. But if love is thick, parents can make occasional mistakes and children will bounce right back. They are so convinced of their parents' love that nothing can jar them.

Take my husband, Jan, for example. He grew up in a very restrictive home in Europe. His parents knew what was best for him. They had ideals that they wanted him to reach, and when he deviated from the straight and narrow, he got it. But the amazing thing is, he doesn't remember the punishments. It was only recently, when his sisters were reminiscing about their childhood, that they brought up the subject of how hard their dad had been on Jan. He was surprised to learn that he got whipped almost nightly during soccer season because he was so busy playing that he would forget to come home until after bedtime. The girls remember pleading his case, but it didn't do much good. Dad was firm and believed the pain of corporal punishment would eventually make his son shape up. Sometimes Jan was punished twice for his misdeeds: at school if he misbehaved or didn't get his lessons done, and then get a second spanking at home.

You would think that with all those spankings Jan would have a warped personality, or would at least remember the harsh punishment. But he doesn't! I believe the reason is that Jan experienced so much love during his childhood that the negatives lost their impact. Through it all, Jan never doubted that his parents loved him. And he also knew he richly deserved the punishment he got.

All parents make mistakes. Some, like Jan's father, are so restrictive that it sometimes borders on harshness. Others may be too permissive, and children have to learn bitter lessons by trial and error. But why do so many of these children hold no resentment? Ask them, and I think you'll find it's because they have always felt loved.

But this fact poses a problem in today's busy society. The bottom line is that children don't feel loved unless they receive adequate positive attention. But it's impossible to show attention without spending time doing things together. Therefore, many children today feel unloved because their parents are too busy. Thus, parents don't have the luxury of making very many mistakes with their children.

That's why there's such an emphasis on democratic government within the home, on understanding children, and on positive techniques of communication. You can't afford to be too restrictive or too permissive. If you're not spending much time together, you can't afford to take any chances that your child will get the wrong message about love.

Why don't you start today building that love cushion, so that when you make a mistake—as we all do—it won't destroy your child. Instead, he or she will be able to bounce back on that cushion of love and say without a doubt, "But I know my folks still love me."

Later research has taken these four basic parental groups and has looked more closely at the variables of love and support. Basically they found that those parents who were high in both love and support—the *authoritative* ones—were the most likely to have well-adjusted children. These children had the highest self-worth scores and were the least involved in antisocial behavior such as gangs, truancy, drugs, and promiscuity.

This might be expected, because these children knew their parents loved and believed in them. But what might be surprising is how the other three types of parenting styles ranked: The *permissive* parents, who showed love but not much support, ranked second. The *neglectful* and *authoritarian* parents, who were low in love, came in last.

What parenting styles resulted in children who related best to authority figures? Again, *authoritative* parents were the highest, followed by *permissive* ones. *Neglectful* parents came next, with *authoritarian* parents ranking last. High control with little love is the parenting style that fosters the highest levels of disobedience.

In all categories the *authoritative* parenting style with high love and high support was the most effective. Again it was the love, in spite of the child's behavior, that seemed to be the most important factor. These parents also tended to communicate their expectations in a reasonable and winsome way. The bottom line is that when parents are loving and supportive, the result is easy obedience!

Balancing love and authority

Effective discipline depends on a parent's ability to balance love and authority, the ability to be tender and tough. It is great to have fun with your children, to laugh over silly things and to play crazy games, but children can sometimes carry these activities to extremes. At that moment you may have to say firmly, "That is enough!" At other times you must follow a strict admonition with a hug to show that all is forgiven and forgotten.

One evening Jan told our school-age daughters to settle down and go to sleep. But they continued talking, joking, and laughing. He told them again, but they didn't listen. Finally he sighed and nudged me, "OK, Kay. It's your turn."

I marched into their room in military style and commanded, "That is enough. Be quiet this minute and go to sleep." Instantly the room was still. As I turned to march out again, I stopped and asked in a different tone, "Did you girls say your prayers?"

"No," they replied.

"Then you had better say them right now!" I said firmly.

Obediently each girl knelt down, and Kari earnestly prayed, "Dear Jesus, please help my mommy not to be so strict."

The irony of the situation was too much, and all three of us burst out laughing. After prayers, we hugged and kissed and parted friends.

A good disciplinarian constantly walks a tightrope between tender and tough—between love and authority. Sometimes you may tip in one direction, but you correct the error with a little tip in the opposite direction. You are not afraid to be the authority when needed, but you are equally unafraid to show love and affection.

The balancing act works best when love and authority are blended into a total approach—when you can say kindly but firmly, "I mean what I say." Harsh, unreasonable demands have no place in the repertoire of an effective disciplinarian. But if you do act harshly on occasion, an apology and a little love help to heal the hurt.

Qualities of effective disciplinarians

There are five qualities you should incorporate into your parenting style that will help you build the cushion of love that is essential for easy obedience: You must be open and approachable; maintain an even emotional temperature; be consistent; maintain a united front; and let God's Word guide your actions.

Open and approachable. Approachable people are open to new ideas; they are willing to listen and will seriously consider another person's (even a little person's) suggestions, criticism, needs, concerns, demands, and wishes before making a decision, rather than jealously guarding decision-making as their parental right.

Honesty is the first step to being an open, approachable parent. An honest parent can admit mistakes, lack of knowledge, or embarrassment. When children know that their parents will be truthful and will listen without criticism or laughter, a rapport develops that enhances a child's willingness to obey.

Parents may be open in one area while closed in another, depending on their own backgrounds. Children quickly learn when and how to approach their parents. They also learn the issues to avoid. Being an open parent is especially vital in the area of sex education. Children will feel comfortable coming to their parents with their questions or problems only if their parents don't skirt the issues, act embarrassed, pretend that they don't know, or are too busy to explain.

Parents who are dictatorial are usually closed individuals. Being closed is a defense mechanism learned in childhood. People don't like to be made fun of, so they hide their feelings; they don't like to be criticized, so they hide their talents; they don't like their positions to be threatened, so they cut themselves off from anyone who might challenge them—or they exert their authority and put the challenger down.

When family leadership is closed, it leads to poor morale in the ranks; discontent can grow, and rebellion is often the result. Some parents feel that a closed form of family government is preferable during early childhood. But total control is different from a benevolent dictatorship, in which parents are in control but must keep open to the needs of those they are responsible to in order to continue cushioning them with love.

Even young children feel resentful when their suggestions and wishes are ignored and when they are not allowed to make the little decisions they are capable of making. Children also resent parents who can't admit a mistake or change their ways, but require perfection from every family member under 18.

Maintain an even emotional temperature in front of your children. Lukewarm may be a distasteful temperature for milk or root beer, but it's just right for parents. When parents are emotionally too cold or too hot, they are not very much fun to be around. On the cold side they are rejecting and neglecting. On the hot side they are quick-tempered and explosive. Many parents believe that anger is the only way to compel obedience, but this is not so. Children do not obey because of anger. They obey because they know that anger leads to swift and decisive punitive action, so they obey out of fear.

It is far better to take the time to handle misbehavior immediately, rather than let your temperature continue to rise until you act emotionally and give your children a model of aggressive behavior.

When parents reach a boiling point, when emotions sour, their bodies are ready for immediate action—either to fight or to flee. And too many parents choose to fight! Thinking becomes irrational; demeaning words fly, and it is easy for parents to strike out physically at the object of their frustration. Child abuse, both verbal and physical, is too often the result of letting one's emotional temperature reach the boiling point. Therefore, I suggest that you live by the following principle: *Never discipline in anger.*

Angry words and aggressive actions are two of the easiest behaviors to model or imitate. You will have enough trouble coping with your children's anger and aggression. Don't give them any reason to say they learned their uncontrolled emotional reactions from you.

Be aware of your feelings, and don't bottle them up. When you sense that your emotional temperature is beginning to rise, do something about it immediately. Don't wait to reach the point of explosion. If your child needs immediate attention, take a deep breath, think coolly, and keep your voice low. If you're dangerously close to explosion, walk around the block, attack the dirty garage, yank out the weeds, play tennis, call your spouse, or pray before interacting with your child. When you have brought your temperature under control, it is much easier to think of creative ways to solve the problem. And when your emotions are under control, it's easier for your children to control theirs too.

If you are thinking it's impossible to never discipline when you're angry, look again at what Jesus said in Mark 10:27: "With men it is impossible, but not with God: for with God all things are possible." Jesus wasn't speaking specifically of being able to overcome anger before disciplining, but I think the application is appropriate. If it seems impossible to control your anger to such an extent that you will never discipline in anger, then it probably is, if you try to do it by yourself. *But nothing is impossible with God.* Make a habit of stepping away from the discipline of your children long enough to pray for God's help to control your anger before dealing with them. Give God a chance to help you keep control.

When you're upset, say to your children—who are probably also upset—"Kids, I'm ready to haul off and hit you. I need God's help to control my anger and give me some creative ideas of how to discipline you so this will never happen again. Please give me a few minutes to go to my room and pray." (Or you may want to pray with them.)

Do you realize what that statement will say to your children? First of all, that whatever they did was a major offense and deserves major punishment. Therefore, anything short of their worst expectations is going to be seen as a direct answer to prayer. Plus, they know that you and God are in this thing together, and that's an unbeatable team. They might as well surrender now rather than try to fight!

When they hear you ask for time out to pray, they are probably going to say, "That's a great idea. Pray as long as you need to. And we'll also be praying that God can impress you to be reasonable."

One parent who used this method, specifically when she felt that a spanking was in order because of her children's willful defiance, said that as soon as she went into her room to pray, her children's attitudes changed. Many times, by the time she came out they were sorry for what they had done and apologized, so there was no longer a need to give the punishment she had planned to deliver. How much better if a haughty, willful spirit can be broken by prayer rather than by punishment.

There are two warnings I must give, however, about the use of prayer. First, don't use prayer as a way to "sanctify" the punishment you already have decided to deliver so you won't feel guilty. When you pray, be open to the Holy Spirit's ideas and intervention, and be willing to change directions if that is what's indicated. And second, don't make God the bad guy. Don't blame the Lord for your punitive actions by saying something such as "I'm doing this because God told me not to spare the rod!" Words similar to this can cause children to have negative feelings about God, which then interferes with their lifelong relationship with Him.

When you err, and hasty, uncontrolled words escape your lips, or when you impulsively grab or slap your child, apologize immediately. Children are resilient and seldom hold grudges if it is a rare occurrence *and* they know that Mom and Dad are truly sorry *and* if they can see that

Mom and Dad are making a genuine effort to be better parents. Determine what caused you to fly off the handle and work on eliminating the cause.

Many parents were raised in homes in which anger was used to control people. You may feel as though you spend much of your time fighting the urge to do the same. You may at times feel helpless in the face of your own uncontrollable rage. People who have family tendencies toward quick anger must deal with this issue almost daily. In recognizing that most parents have trouble with anger, you are not excusing yourself. Instead, you are allowing yourself to be human. Guilt won't help an angry person. It just adds to the pressures that tend to make human pressure cookers explode. So don't lay a guilt trip on yourself. Just as children are resilient and forgiving, so is God. You must also forgive yourself.

If anger and losing control are frequent issues for you, then you need to ask why. For some it is because of a dysfunctional family background. Research has shown that those who are most likely to abuse their children are people who were themselves abused when they were young. If this is your case, you can break the cycle.

You also need to look at your current lifestyle. Is there too much pressure on you? Can you rearrange things (commitments, responsibilities) in your life to take off some of the pressure? Are you temporarily in a very demanding situation that will end soon? Can you keep in mind that the situation is temporary and then try to take things easier and relax more? Are you upset about something deep down and haven't recognized it yet? Ask yourself if there are emotional issues you need to deal with so that you'll have more patience with your children.

Also take a look at your children. Some children, such as strong-willed, hyperactive, or handicapped ones, are more difficult to raise than others. The more difficult the child, the more encouragement and support you may need from others to help you maintain a positive attitude and demeanor. Otherwise frustration and anger may become overwhelming. Don't be afraid to reach out for help. You need time off from your children so you can come back refreshed. The more difficult the child, the more time off you need.

Finally, especially if you feel you have physically or psychologically injured your child, you need to find help and support. With Christ's help you can change. Although change may take time, it will come. Abusive behavior is usually committed in private, while in public your behavior is exemplary. That's why your closest friends, if you try to talk about your anger problem, might not believe you and may unintentionally make the problem worse by denying it: "You couldn't have done that." Find someone who will listen to you and understand. Hundreds of thousands of parents, many of whom are practicing Christians, are struggling just like you.

You may be able to find a support group of parents with similar problems in your vicinity. Check with your pediatrician for names of such groups. The organization Parents Anonymous sponsors local groups around the country. They provide parents with the mutual encouragement they need to work on their problems of potential or actual abuse.

I've generally found that the most satisfied and effective parents are those who have a good support system—grandmas, uncles, cousins, and friends who are willing to help whenever needed—to give parents time off to pull themselves together. Make sure your support network is strong.

Be consistent. Let's pretend that you think it is very important for your child to make her bed each morning. She knows the rule. But you are busy and often forget to check her room until after she's gone to school. Or if you check and the bed's unmade, you sometimes feel that it's easier to ignore the infraction than to exert the extra effort needed to get her to obey before the school bus arrives. Then by the time you both get home after school, the bed is forgotten.

Now, you still feel strongly about the bed, and you have communicated this to your child in no uncertain terms. Shouldn't this be enough to get the job done? She clearly knows what she should do. Why doesn't she do it? The reason is that this requirement has not been *consistently* enforced.

Inconsistency produces a 50-50 decision-maker. This is what happens: Junior wakes up in the morning and yawns. "Let's see," he says as he tumbles out of bed, "shall I make my bed this morning? Well, chances are 50-50 that Mom won't even notice, and I really don't feel like doing it. So . . . I think I'll take a chance and leave it unmade."

But if Mom consistently enforced and reinforced the type of behavior she expected from her child until this behavior became ingrained and habitual, the scenario would be different. Junior would wake up in the morning and say, "Let's see, shall I make my bed?" Then he would weigh the alternatives ("If I don't, Mom will make me do it before breakfast") and make a wise decision ("I guess I'd better go ahead and get it over with").

Children will abide by reasonable requirements and limitations, but their tendency is to do as little as possible. Even 2-year-olds will try to get away with as much as they can. They'll quickly learn that even though their parents say no frequently, the limits will come tumbling down if they kick hard enough. When their persistent challenging meets with parental inconsistency, they'll be encouraged to kick at every limit they don't like.

Consistency in parental behavior checks this testing behavior in the young child before it becomes habitual. After all, kicking against too many firm, solid rules takes a lot of energy and can cause pain. Therefore, children become much more careful about the limits they choose to test, and become better able to discipline themselves.

Maintain a united front. It is sometimes difficult to be consistent when Dad, Mom, Grandpa, your cousin Jim, Aunt Mildred, and the baby-sitter are all involved in parenting. When there are several parental figures, the child often becomes frustrated by conflicting messages.

As children develop, it is important to learn to relate to a wide number of adults and cope with their differences of opinion. But children also need consistency and order in their own homes. It is very important that adults responsible for a young child reach a consensus about their requirements and support each other in this decision. Undermining an absent parent or another authority figure plants seeds of disrespect in a child's fertile mind.

If parents and/or parental figures are in conflict about disciplinary tactics, children will take full advantage of this opportunity and play one adult against the other in order to get their own way. This causes more family conflict. If parents have differences of opinion about rearing a child, these should be resolved privately. When children are confronted, they should meet a united front. Otherwise, parents beware! Children do not have to take lessons to learn how to divide and conquer.

The role one parent plays with the children can significantly influence the role the other plays. For example, one parent often tends to balance the love or authority shown by the other. Especially when you're overbearing with your kids, you may be forcing your spouse to lean significantly in the other direction and become overly permissive and nurturant.

Think back to your childhood. Does this scene sound vaguely familiar?

Dad's been away all day, hard at work. Mom's been working hard at home. She was there when the children got home. She heard all about the little squabbles at school and the huge homework assignments. The children had had a tough day, so she didn't push the chores. They needed a little diversion, a little time of their own. But before she knew it, Dad was walking up the drive. "Kids," she calls, "Dad's home. You'd better get your chores done or you'll get it."

The children dash off to do what they were supposed to do, but it's too late. Dad walks in, takes one look around, and notices the trash hasn't been emptied, the leaves haven't been raked, and the tools are still scattered all over the garage. At supper Dad lays down the law and dishes out the consequences for shirking responsibilities.

Mom tries to take the children's side. "It's my fault. I didn't remind them, and they needed some free time." But Dad is determined, and nothing will change his mind.

That night as Mom makes the rounds for a hug and kiss and bedtime prayers, she lingers to listen and to patch up the hard feelings the children have because they've been bossed around and pressured into doing things they don't want to do.

Have you experienced this balancing effect? When one parent is overbearing and comes down hard, often the other parent will react in just the opposite direction.

Children need authority and love from each parent. It's too bad when the behavior of one parent forces the other to act just the opposite, especially when the other would rather present a more balanced approach.

Too often the result is resentment, hard feelings, and open conflict.

It's as if parents are on a seesaw. If they both stay close to the middle—being both strong and loving—then they tend to have a close, supportive relationship with each other. But if one gets too far out on the edge and becomes overbearingly authoritarian or neglectfully permissive, it forces the other parent to move in the opposite direction to keep the seesaw balanced. The result is that parents move away from each other. If you've ever played on a seesaw you realize the danger: One finally moves so far out that he or she falls off the end, causing the other to hit the dirt with a thud.

I hope your seesaw is balanced. If not, maybe you and your mate had better talk about what you are doing to each other and make a valiant attempt to put your act together!

Let God's Word guide your actions. Most of all, let your parenting style reflect biblical principles. Proverbs is a good place to start your search. You'll find gems such as:

- "Trust in the Lord with all your heart.
  And lean not on your own understanding;
  In all your ways acknowledge Him,
  And He shall direct your paths" (3:5, 6).
- "For whom the Lord loves He corrects,
  Just as a father the son in whom he delights" (verse 12).
- "He who walks with integrity walks securely,
  But he who perverts his ways will become known" (10:9).
- "A man of understanding holds his peace" (11:12).
- "The generous soul will be made rich,
  And he who waters will also be watered himself" (verse 25).
- "He who spares his rod hates his son,
  But he who loves him disciplines him promptly" (13:24).
- "The wise woman builds her house,
  But the foolish pulls it down with her hands" (14:1).
- "He who is slow to wrath has great understanding,
  But he who is impulsive exalts folly" (verse 29).
- "Without counsel, plans go awry,
  But in the multitude of counselors they are established" (15:22).
- "A word spoken in due season, how good it is!" (verse 23).
- "Pride goes before destruction,
  And a haughty spirit before a fall" (16:18).
- "Better is a dry morsel with quietness,
  Than a house full of feasting with strife" (17:1).

- "A merry heart does good, like medicine,
  But a broken spirit dries the bones" (verse 22).
- "Listen to counsel and receive instruction,
  That you may be wise in your latter days" (19:20).
- "It is honorable for a man to stop striving,
  Since any fool can start a quarrel" (20:3).
- "The righteous man walks in his integrity;
  His children are blessed after him" (verse 7).
- "Whoever curses his father or his mother,
  His lamp will be put out in deep darkness" (verse 20).
- "Better to dwell in a corner of a housetop,
  Than in a house shared with a contentious woman" (21:9).
- "By humility and the fear of the Lord
  Are riches and honor and life" (22:4).
- "Train up a child in the way he should go,
  And when he is old he will not depart from it" (verse 6).
- "Listen to your father who begot you,
  And do not despise your mother when she is old" (23:22).
- "Through wisdom a house is built,
  And by understanding it is established;
  By knowledge the rooms are filled
  With all precious and pleasant riches" (24:3, 4).
- "Where there is no wood, the fire goes out;
  And where there is no talebearer, strife ceases" (26:20).
- "He who tills his land will have plenty of bread,
  But he who follows frivolity will have poverty enough!" (28:19).

Read again and again Psalm 37:4-8: "Delight yourself also in the Lord, and He shall give you the desires of your heart. Commit your way to the Lord, trust also in Him. . . . Cease from anger, and forsake wrath; do not fret—it only causes harm." Hold fast to the promise that God will give you the desires of your heart. Many times your impulsive, rash behavior can be tempered by the realization that God wants the best for you. Trust Him. Give your life to Him, and look forward with eager anticipation for His promise to be fulfilled.

The research referred to in this chapter can be found in Martin L. Hoffman and Lois Wladis Hoffman, eds., *Review of Child Development Research* (New York: Russell Sage Foundation, 1964), vol. 1, p. 198; Dennis Guernsey, "What Kind of a Parent Are You?" *Family Life Today,* January 1976; and Diana Baumrind, "Effects of Authoritative Parental Control on Child Behavior," *Child Development* 37 (1966): 887-907.

Chapter 4

Attention and the Love Cup Principle

Blessed are those parents who are teachable, for knowledge brings understanding, and understanding brings love.—Old Union Reminder.

The most common reason children misbehave is to get attention. When children, as well as adults, get positive attention, they feel loved. Without it life is empty and meaningless. That's why children will often resort to whatever it takes to get attention. Destructive behavior, threats of suicide, and blatant disobedience are often merely the way the child has chosen to cry "Won't someone pay attention to me?" Attention is so important that a child would rather have negative attention than no attention at all.

Love is essential for a child's healthy development. During World War II studies of babies in orphanages disclosed that some children failed to develop properly. After a year or two some children were not sitting or walking, and some even died. Why? They had enough food, each one had a crib, and their diapers were changed regularly. But one essential ingredient for growth was missing. No one touched, cuddled, or rocked them. No one gave them positive attention. Children cannot live without love. Nobody loved them. Their love cups were empty.

Love is also important for changing negative behavior into positive behavior. In fact, giving love can be a more effective behavior changer than using time-out, restrictions, and other consequences that are considered more typical discipline! When children need the type of positive attention that makes them feel loved, no amount of punishment, threats, bribes, anger, or spankings is going to effectively solve the behavior problem. The child in fear may cease his or her disobedience for a time, but if the basic need for love is unmet, the disobedience will soon surface again. The only thing that will effectively stop misbehavior that is caused by the need for attention is to meet the need as soon as possible so the child is not rewarded for negative behavior.

The love cup principle makes the relationship between love and misbehavior more graphic. Children are like cups. When they are filled to overflowing, they have enough love to give away, they can be loving to you and others, and they will tend to behave in an acceptable manner.

Children equate love with attention. So when children feel empty, they will try to fill themselves with attention, and too often this bid for attention results in obnoxious behavior—showing off, putting others down, blaming, criticizing, fighting, arguing, and destructive actions.

The concept is revolutionary: You have the power to change your children's misbehavior by simply filling their love cups. The story of Lori illustrates how the love cup principle works.

Seven-year-old Lori was having a miserable day. She whined, pouted, pushed her little sister, Lisa, and then grabbed away Lisa's favorite doll.

Finally Mother could stand it no longer. "Lori, what has gotten into you? You'd better straighten up and be kind to your sister, or you're going to get it!"

Lori paid no attention to the threat and continued to say mean things to Lisa. At bedtime Mother told Lori that her words were so sour that she felt like making Lori suck a lemon so she could understand just how sour they were. That made Lori even more angry. "You like Lisa more than you like me," Lori retorted. She fell asleep sulking.

The next morning Lori woke up in a bad mood. She complained miserably when Mother attempted to comb out the tangles in her hair. Mother was beside herself; what was wrong with Lori?

Then she remembered a book she had read about the love cup. Could Lori be suffering from a lack of positive attention? Mother called, "Lori, I think I know what's wrong with you."

"You do?" Lori looked puzzled.

"Yes," said her mother. "I think your love cup is empty! Come over here and let me fill it up."

Mom sat Lori on her lap, hugged and kissed her, and told her how special she was. Lori was surprised, but she obviously enjoyed the attention. She knew she deserved the opposite. After a minute, Mom asked Lori if her love cup was filled.

"No, but it's up to here," said Lori, as she pointed to her chest.

Mother loved her up again. Then she asked, "Is it full now?"

"No," said Lori, "but it's up to my chin."

"Good," said Mother, with a big hug. "Let's see if we can't get that cup so full that it will spill right over the top."

Finally, with a big smile on her face, Lori said that she was full and running over.

"Well, if you've got that much love," said Mother, "why don't you give some of it to your sister?"

"Oh, no," said Lori, "Lisa will just push me away." Mother knew that after the obnoxious way Lori had treated Lisa, that just might happen. But she encouraged Lori to waste a little love on her sister, since she had so much it was overflowing. Somewhat hesitantly Lori went up to Lisa and said, "Lisa, I love you," and gave her a hug. Lisa hugged her sister back, tightly. Then they both headed off hand in hand to the breakfast table.

But that's not the end of the story. A few weeks later Mother had a terrible day. She grumbled and spoke harshly to the girls. After a while Lori said, "Mommy, I think I know what's wrong with you. Your love cup is empty!" Then she threw her arms around her mom's neck and gave her a big kiss. Do you know what happened to Mother's love cup? Just like that, it filled to overflowing, and Mom was her happy self again.

Meeting a child's need for positive attention is the most basic way to both prevent and solve behavior problems. Noted child psychiatrist Rudolf Dreikurs, in his book *Children: The Challenge,* suggests that attention is the number one reason children misbehave. When a child's need for attention is not met positively, he or she will continue to misbehave, and chances are this will lead to the second reason for misbehavior—a struggle for power between the child and authority figures.

The majority of a child's "healthy" misbehavior occurs on these two planes, starting with a need for attention and moving into a need for power and control. Creative disciplinarians will continually work with their children in these areas to keep them from moving on to more pathological misbehavior caused by wanting revenge and feeling inadequate or inferior.

Because the need for attention is the basic cause of misbehavior, creative disciplinarians must be masters at recognizing when their children's love cups are empty and be willing to fill them immediately. Full cups mean behavior problems are kept to a minimum. But when empty, children try to fill themselves by trying to get more attention. They seek approval; they try to be good. But how often do good children get much attention? Not often. Most children find that they get more attention by being bad—by showing off, acting silly, being destructive, or getting into mischief. Getting attention sometimes becomes such an overwhelming need that children cease to care if it is positive or negative. Being yelled at or beaten is better than being ignored.

I hope your child doesn't have to misbehave in order to get your attention. But has something like this ever happened to you? You just got home from work. It's been a hard day. You're exhausted. You kick off your shoes, flop down on the couch, and begin leafing through the paper. You're particularly interested in what happened on the stock market during the day. Just as you begin to scan the columns, your little 3-year-old comes running up to you saying, "Daddy, Daddy, come outside and see what I made."

What do you do? Say "Sure, honey, I'll be glad to," and then put your shoes back on and follow your child outside? Is that what you would do? Not if you're like most parents! Most of us would say something like this: "Not now; can't you see I'm reading the paper?"

And what does your child do? Retreat and silently wait for you to finish the paper? No, this is the typical scenario:

"Daddy, please, I can't wait! I want to show you . . ."

"Well, you better wait, because I'm busy."

"Daddy, let me show you," your child pleads, taking hold of the edge of the paper and wiggling it.

"Let go of the paper! I can't read with you jerking it up and down. Now get out of here and let me finish."

"But, Daddy . . ."

You cut off his pleading by saying, "If you don't give me a little peace and quiet, then I'll give you just what you deserve. Out with you."

And with the threat of impending danger, your child retreats to the other room. But only for a few minutes.

The child hasn't seen you all day, and his love cup is almost empty. Since children equate love with attention, the child isn't satisfied until he gets the attention he needs so desperately. So what does Johnny do? Well, he takes a flying leap and jumps right into the middle of the paper, tearing it up.

Now what do you do? Give him what he richly deserves? Or do you give him what he so urgently needs?

Most of us just don't understand the subtle (and sometimes not so subtle) messages that our children are trying to give us. Most of us see this obnoxious behavior of a child as just an ornery streak that needs to be corrected with punishment, when the real message is "Daddy, my love cup is empty and needs to be filled with a little positive attention—and I can't wait!"

So be prepared. The next time you're reading the paper and your little one comes up and needs a little extra attention, put your paper down, take your child on your lap, or go see what the child wants you to see. Chances are that in a couple minutes your child's love cup will be full with enough positive attention that you'll be able to go back and read your paper again. I'll guarantee that you'll enjoy that stock market report a whole lot more by giving love and attention first. And you won't have to put up with a disobedient child.

Remember the love cup principle the next time someone you know becomes obnoxious. When a cup is empty, nothing will change that offensive behavior quite as quickly as a little extra love—positive attention. Spend some fun time together, encourage your child, or share some words of appreciation. See if it doesn't make a difference and reduce your child's need for negative behavior.

One young mother learned about the love cup principle at one of my seminars. She remained skeptical, but her 5-year-old David was so unruly that she was desperate, ready to try anything. So for a few weeks she patiently filled his love cup. The change was nearly miraculous! David didn't become an angel; he was still an active 5-year-old. But his rebellion disappeared. Gradually he became a happy, responsive, cooperative child.

But David's mother found a new conflict. Her revised child-rearing method caused a problem with her parents. They disapproved. They subscribed to the idea of "spare the rod and spoil the child." Slowly she reverted to her old habits—yelling and spanking. David responded in kind, reverting to his old self—obstinate, challenging, and disagreeable.

Later David's mother reviewed the seminar material and decided the love cup principle was worth another try. In two weeks she wrote to me: "It works. Love really works. My happy, gentle, and fun-loving boy is back again. I'll never again let anyone talk me into emptying his love cup."

Hundreds of parents like David's mother have shared with me similar experiences they have had with the power of love to change lives. I've recorded those stories in the book *Cherishing Your Child.* Love is foundational for all parenting. In fact, you can discipline only as much as you are willing to love.

The love cup principle will work with your child, too. I know it will. Won't you give it a try? I have a feeling someone in your life could use a little filling right now!

Chapter 5

Power and the String Strategy

"And now a word to you parents. Don't keep on scolding and nagging your children, making them angry and resentful. Rather, bring them up with the loving discipline the Lord himself approves, with suggestions and godly advice" (Eph. 6:4, TLB).

The second reason children misbehave is because they want power. They want to control their own lives, make decisions, do what they want to do. And when they get into power struggles with their parents and other authority figures, they want to win. They seldom give up the fight easily. That's why easy obedience focuses on preventing conflict, or if conflict does arise, solving it so it doesn't surface again. The fewer the conflicts, the fewer power struggles there will be in your family, and the easier obedience will be.

Children are born with a will that must be molded, or they will be misfits in society and a threat to others—or themselves. Some people believe that children are born either compliant or defiant. That's not true. Rather, children are born with varied characteristics, some of which are easier to live with than others.

When a number of more difficult characteristics are seen in the personality and behavior of children, the parental tendency is to try to force them into behaving more like the "perfect" children parents want them to be. The more you push your expectations upon them rather than respecting their God-given characteristics, the more resistant they become to change—and the more defiant. It's as the chemist Morris Moen once said: "To use a computer analogy, each child is born with its own individual hardware. It is up to the parents to figure out (without a manual) which software works for what child. You will not have good results trying to raise a Macintosh child using IBM programs."

Parents are the cause of much of the defiant behavior in children. I can best illustrate what I mean with a string, because children are like strings.

Take a string and stretch it out in front of you. Now take one end and push the string forward, against itself. Does the string move straight in the direction you're pushing? No, of course not. It buckles up. And if you keep pushing, you will soon have a wadded-up string. But try pulling the string the way you want it to go, and it will follow.

Children are like strings; they tend to resist when they feel pushed or forced into doing something. Once they start to resist, the tendency of most parents is to push them all the more, to threaten, to manipulate, to force, and to punish. And the consequence is, the more you push, the more powerless the child feels, and therefore the more rebellious.

There may be times you think pushing or forcing a child results in compliance. But in too many cases it's like the little boy whose dad told him to sit down in church. When the boy kept jumping up, his dad physically pushed the kid into his seat with the command "I said *sit down!*"

The little boy sat there, but a few minutes later he could be heard muttering, "I may be sitting on the outside, but I'm standing on the inside!"

Outward compliance accomplished by force doesn't necessarily mean inner compliance, and sooner or later inner defiance causes outward defiance!

The key to diminishing a child's stubborn resistance is to remember just how much children and strings are alike. If you push them in the direction you want them to go, they won't do it.

Using the string strategy of not pushing your child should begin at birth by respecting the child's rights as a human being. Don't rudely interrupt babies by snatching away a rattle, sticking a bottle in their mouths, or picking them up as if they were rag dolls and had no feelings. Don't impose your will on babies just because they have no choice.

Instead, slow down. Observe your baby. If the child is interested in something, respect that. Talk to your infant, even though he or she can't answer yet. When you must pick your child up, you could say, "Are you ready to go with Mommy? I'll pick you up now."

Prepare infants for changes you are going to be imposing on them. Get their attention. Tell them what you are going to do. If it's changing diapers, keep up a running commentary on your actions; this will capture their full attention. You'll notice the wiggling—the resistance—will disappear! Then say, "Thank you for being so cooperative," and reward them for compliance. Give them an extra snuggle and kiss. Rewarding children for compliance is a lot better than forcing your will on them and then having to punish them for defiance.

If you show genuine respect, you will have a much better chance of winning your child's cooperation from day one. I challenge you to try it. See if it doesn't make a difference!

As children grow older, how should stubborn resistance be handled? Go back to the string. If you want that string to move in a certain direction, don't push it. Take the opposite end and pull—I mean lead—and the string will follow!

Any time a child begins to resist, even slightly, remember the string and immediately quit pushing. Instead, step back a few paces and consider creative ways to lead your child in the direction you want him or her to go. If nothing else, acknowledge your child's feelings and ask for cooperation: "I can tell you don't like what I've told you to do. But it really needs to be done. What would it take to make the task more attractive to you?"

Respect your child's rights, but don't let that child step on yours. As members of your family and as citizens, children have certain responsibilities. Your job is to motivate, encourage, guide, and gently influence your children so they will choose to fulfill those responsibilities and do what you want them to do.

And what if children don't choose to obey? That's where consequences come in—and creative disciplinary techniques that are found in this book. But in most cases, if you don't get into a tug of wills, your child will come around to your way of thinking or you will reach an acceptable compromise. Keep your emotions under control and take the necessary time to resolve the conflict.

Motivating, encouraging, guiding, and influencing do take time, but they are worth it in order to have the child willingly comply with your requests rather than stubbornly resist everything you say, or make decisions based on an attitude of rebellion. Willful defiance too often leads to experimentation with harmful practices, such as smoking pot, using drugs, participating in premarital sex, or running away from home. Rebellious children think they are hurting you by their defiant behavior, but in reality they are hurting themselves far more!

So, don't push the string. Instead, here are some ways to lead your children in the way you want them to go:

1. Make requests when your child is not deeply absorbed in some favorite activity. Children don't like to be interrupted any more than adults do.

2. Give your child fair warning that a change is about to take place: "You have 10 minutes before you need to put away your blocks. I'll set the timer."

3. Ask for cooperation: "I really need your help to set the table." "It would make me happy to have you work with me." "If you help me now, I'll be able to help you with your science project later."

4. When possible, give your child a choice: "I've listed three things that have to be done before we go shopping. Which task would you rather do?"

5. Work together happily. Children enjoy doing what you're doing—if you're fun to be around.

6. Use humor, games, and playacting to hurdle potential conflicts. Play beauty shop when combing tangled hair. Play restaurant with finicky eaters. Reverse your roles when the house needs cleaning—and let the child tell you what to do. (For more ideas, see the chapter entitled "Playing Problems Away.")

7. Encourage! Encourage! Encourage! Remember, it's a discouraged child who most often misbehaves. You can turn defiance into compliance if you just remember the string strategy!

When parents err

Many power struggles result because parents have made a foolish or untimely request, spouted off something they didn't really mean, and their children sense the unfairness and make a good case for not having to obey. The way parents deal with their own mistakes has a lot to do with either continued respect and rapport between parents and children, or the breakdown of the relationship.

Too many parents, knowing consistency is important, won't admit they have made a mistake. They continue to push, and end up with major rebellion. Here's an example: Joyce was rushing to feed her children early so she could come to my parenting class that started at 7:00 in the evening. Her 3-year-old daughter, Emmy, was a finicky eater and often refused to eat anything, causing incredible frustration on Joyce's part. Because of this history, the red flags should have been flying around the supper table.

Parents need to choose their battles carefully. It takes time to solve a power struggle effectively. It takes time to apply the string strategy and figure out a way to lead a child in the way you want that child to go. It takes time to establish a win-win situation for both parents and children. So if you don't have the time, you need to consider carefully whether the situation is worth a battle. Just as on a real battlefield, so it is with parenting: you can win the battle—and lose the war. You can force your will on the child, but end up losing the child's respect and having a royal rebellion when the child is 16 years of age—if not before.

Without thinking clearly, Joyce said, "Emmy, eat your dinner now."

Emmy replied in her characteristic way: "No! I don't want to eat."

Frustrated, Mom replied, "You must at least drink your milk."

Again Emmy made her position clear: "No!"

Joyce went over to Emmy, picked up her glass of milk, and demanded, "I said, drink it!"

Emmy held her ground: "No!"

Now what should Joyce do? The battle lines are drawn. The issue is clear. The question is: Should this battle be fought? Here is where those three questions concerning your goals for disciplining need to be asked:

1. Will what I do help my child to become self-disciplined?
2. Will what I do prevent or resolve conflict?
3. Will what I do preserve or build my child's feelings of self-worth?

Without asking these questions and thinking through what was likely to result from her behavior, Joyce gave an ultimatum: "Drink this milk, or else!"

Emmy grabbed the glass and with one wild swing sprayed the contents of the glass all over the kitchen. Joyce screamed, roughly grabbed

Emmy out of her chair, and carried the screaming, kicking child to her bedroom, uttering another foolish ultimatum: "You can just stay there until you are willing to drink your milk." Of course, Joyce didn't mean this, but by this time she already had lost the battle. Was Joyce going to patrol the bedroom door, making sure little Emmy didn't leave her room until she drank her milk? It might take days! This parent had just made a foolish statement that she couldn't enforce—and Emmy had won.

In retrospect, the battle should have been avoided altogether. Emmy's history of dawdling with her food and refusing to eat should have been a red flag for Joyce to consider whether this was the right time to make a stand and force little Emmy to eat.

But she didn't, and demanded, "At least drink your milk." When Emmy resisted, Joyce should have immediately remembered the string strategy. Resistance is the warning sign that a battle will be fought unless Mom does some fancy maneuvering.

I'd suggest a simple admission of a mistake: "Emmy, I'm sorry. I spoke without thinking. I'm rushed to get to a parenting meeting and I don't want you to be hungry tonight, so I wanted you at least to drink your milk. But you are smart enough to make a good decision. You can choose whether you want to drink your milk. I'll leave it here on the counter. Just remember, there won't be any food in the child-care room while I'm at the meeting."

Note: the battle is avoided—but not the consequence. Emmy now has a choice to become self-controlled rather than other-controlled. And being able to make a choice helps a child feel valuable. The three goals of easy obedience have been met:

1. Becoming more self-disciplined.
2. Preventing or resolving conflict.
3. Maintaining or building self-worth.

And all it took was a simple apology on the part of a parent to admit a mistake.

Some parents fear their children won't respect them when they back down. This is not true. If children know that what you have demanded is unfair, they will respect you for owning up to your mistake and apologizing. And just think of what an incredible example this is for your children to admit their mistakes sometime in the future.

It is also OK on occasion for parents to change their minds. If you ask your child to do something, and immediately you see by your child's body language that a fight is brewing, you can choose to change your request to something you feel would be more compatible with your child's will at that moment. The important thing is not to allow your children to think they are getting by with something, or that because of their negative behavior you have changed your mind. That will only reward their defiance and cause you to have to fight bigger battles in the future. Let me give you an example.

Rees was trying to get 3-year-old Adam into his car seat so they could go to town. "Adam, you need to get into your car seat now so we can go to town."

"I don't want to!" bristled Adam.

"Adam, I said get into the car seat. We have to go," urged Rees.

"No!" was Adam's response.

Rees could see the battle brewing, and considered the options.

Option 1: He could take the time to play a game with Adam: "This is *Apollo 13.* You are the astronaut who is flying this spaceship and the countdown has begun. You've got to get fastened in your space seat before launch or there could be a terrible accident. Hurry. 10 . . . 9 . . . 8 . . . I'll help if you need it. This thing is going to blast off . . ." It would be a very rebellious child that wouldn't go along with that game.

Option 2: Since Toni, his wife, was home, Rees could change his mind and give Adam a choice about whether he wanted to go or not: "Adam, I've changed my mind. You don't have to get in your car seat. You can stay home with Mommy. Aren't you lucky!"

Rees chose option 2, and the minute he suggested staying home, Adam jumped into the car seat and started to buckle himself in.

Children of all ages want the power to control their own lives. They will go to incredible lengths to get their own way. The amazing thing is that many times they might even like to do what an authority asks, but say no just to have the power of control. The key is to give children enough choices over little, inconsequential matters so that their need for power is satisfied. Then they won't be so inclined to fight over the big issues in which parents have no option other than to enforce what they have asked.

Most young children, in an attempt to have some control over their lives, choose one or two daily routines that they tend to resist, such as going to the bathroom, brushing their teeth, getting dressed, going to bed, or taking a bath. When you know your child is likely to resist your request, it is important to give the child a related but inconsequential choice so he or she doesn't resist what must be done.

For example, Becky resists bathtime, so it's important when Mom announces bathtime that she doesn't hesitate after making the request, giving Becky a chance to argue. Instead, Mom says, "Becky, it's bathtime. Do you want bubbles or boats in the bathtub?" Typically Becky becomes so engrossed in making the decision about bubbles or boats that she ceases to resist taking a bath.

To the child, winning means power and control. That's why children want to win. It's OK for children to win. The important thing is that just because your child wins shouldn't mean you lose. For easy obedience and continued positive parent-child rapport it's important to have as many win-win situations as possible.

Timing is crucial when it comes to easy obedience. Don't push when:

- Your child has a chip on his or her shoulder.
- You and/or your child are in a negative mode.

- You don't have time to deal with a power struggle in a positive way.
- You and/or your child are angry.
- Your stress level is maxed out.
- Your child is tired or hungry.
- You've had a power struggle recently and feelings are still raw.

As children grow older and become more capable decision-makers, parental control should shift to self-control. Making this shift is not always easy for the parent who has grown used to making decisions for the child. Some parents who have not solved control issues from their own childhood have a difficult time giving up their control over their children.

One of the first signs of dysfunction in a family is the number and severity of the power struggles parents and children experience. If these struggles are not being resolved satisfactorily, parents should seek help by either taking a good parenting course or getting some family counseling. If power struggles are not solved satisfactorily, it is quite likely that the children will begin making decisions just to rebel or to get back at the person exerting control over them. Revenge is the third reason children misbehave.

Chapter 6

Revenge and Iceberg Psychology

O heavenly Father, make me a better parent. Teach me to understand my children, to listen patiently to what they have to say, and to answer all their questions kindly.—Author Unknown.

Another major reason children misbehave is that they allow their emotions to control their behavior. Rebellious behavior is often the result. They want to get back at the people who they feel are controlling them; they want revenge!

In order to be an effective disciplinarian, every parent should take a refresher course in Iceberg Psychology, because there is a close analogy between iceberg behavior and human behavior. Understanding iceberg behavior can help you know what to do to solve emotionally based behavior problems. In fact, if you can just focus on the negative emotion in the formative stages, there is a good chance it will never have to erupt as inappropriate behavior. This chapter is the course you've been looking for: Iceberg Psychology 101.

A common mistake parents make when disciplining their children is to attack the behavior they don't like rather than taking a few minutes to determine the underlying emotion that is causing the problem. To keep yourself from falling into this trap, you must train yourself to think of an iceberg every time your child does something you don't like.

Let me just review iceberg behavior so you'll know what I'm talking about. There is always much more iceberg under the surface of the water than there is above. Yet when you look at an iceberg, you're not immediately aware of the bottom part. If you try to change the iceberg by chipping away at the top part, the iceberg adjusts itself in the water, and chances are something else will emerge.

This is very similar to children's behavior. Any time parents see some emotionally based behavior they don't like, whether it's destructive actions, sassy or mean words, teasing or hostile actions, it's like the top of the iceberg. The parental tendency is to get rid of the behavior that is offensive. They spank, they yell, or they threaten to try and change that behavior. Sometimes these tactics appear to be successful. The offensive behavior disappears. But if you haven't defused the underlying emotion that caused the behavior, there is a strong chance that some other behavior is likely to surface, and it may be worse than the one you tried to get rid of in the first place.

For example, Bill defiantly sassed his mother. She slapped him and threatened to beat him within an inch of his life if he ever did it again. That seemed to solve the problem. No more sassing. But that afternoon Mom went into her bedroom to get dressed to go shopping. She reached into her drawer to get her pantyhose. To her surprise, she found that the legs had been cut off every pair!

She had managed to squelch one type of misbehavior only to have a more devious type surface. Why? Because Mom failed to get underneath the surface of the original misbehavior and take care of the negative emotion that was causing the sassing.

One day 10-year-old Bruce came home yelling, "I hate my teacher. She's stupid." His face was etched with anger; he threw his books to the floor and once more shouted, "I hate her!"

Mom was shocked by this tirade. She stormed into the room. "Bruce," she said, "I'm ashamed of you. That is no way to talk about your teacher."

"I don't care," retorted Bruce. "She's stupid, and I hate her."

"Enough! I'll not have you talking like that. You shouldn't hate anyone, and I should wash your mouth out with soap for calling someone stupid—especially a teacher. Now pick up those books you've thrown all over the floor."

By this time Bruce was livid with rage. He stormed out of the room and slammed the door.

Knowing the ways of most moms and dads and how angry children sometimes become, I suspect that you have experienced similar situations.

What went wrong with Mom's attempts at disciplining? Mom was trying to solve a problem. Bruce's words "I hate my teacher" were unacceptable to her. She was trying to teach Bruce to respect adults. He needed correction. But her correction only made matters worse. Why?

Let's replay the scene with a few minor changes and see what we can learn. Ten-year-old Bruce came home yelling, "I hate my teacher. She's stupid."

Mom did not approve of Bruce's behavior. She had always taught her child to respect adults and never to call anyone stupid. But she recognized that there was something beneath the surface that was causing this. She began to search for the underlying problem. Watch what happened:

"Wow," said Mom. "You feel angry."

"I'll say I am," retorted Bruce. "My teacher made a fool of me in front of all the class."

"It makes you angry to be embarrassed in front of your friends, doesn't it?"

"Yes, it does." Bruce's face began to relax as he started to pick up the books that he had thrown to the floor. "I can't understand why she picked on me. It wasn't my fault. And I tried to tell her, but she just wouldn't listen." At this point Bruce's anger began to melt. His mother came over and put an arm around him, and tears began to slide down his cheeks. They sat down on the couch, and Bruce unloaded the whole story.

When all had been told, explanations listened to, and emotions defused, Mom asked, "Bruce, how do you think you are going to solve your problem with your teacher?" And for the next 10 minutes Mom and Bruce worked on the problem together. At the end, Mom added, "By the way, Bruce, it never really helps when you get angry. And calling people 'stupid' doesn't solve anything."

"Yeah, I know. I'll try to remember. And thanks for listening."

When it comes to searching for the emotion underneath the misbehavior, the key is to listen, because the only way the troublesome emotion is going to be defused is to be vented by talking about it. What you want to avoid is letting the emotion be acted out in unacceptable ways.

Start listening by acknowledging the emotion you think might be the culprit. "Oh, you feel angry." "You seem sad." "It's scary when something like that happens." Your recognition of your child's emotion gives the message that it's OK to be experiencing it. And immediately your child feels you're an ally. If you guess wrong, your child will correct you. "No, I'm not angry; I'm just disappointed." Then listen as your child expresses the emotion that has been identified.

Continue to listen and acknowledge what your child has said by nodding your head or making comments such as "yes" or "oh." Let your body language express interest as well. Sometimes just being silent is the best invitation for your child to talk.

As you listen, you'll notice something very interesting happening. The strong emotion that caused the misbehavior will begin to dissipate. Then, once that emotion has been defused, your child is ready to move on to solving the problem. At that time you can say, "It's really tough to be in a situation like this, but what do you think you might do about it?" Problem solving is seldom effective when there is too much emotion. Unbiased thinking is impossible in a highly emotional atmosphere.

The way we were brought up, our culture, will determine what we consider as acceptable expressions of emotions. While some families get more heated and may shout and pound their fists, other families prefer a more controlled approach to dealing with troublesome emotions. Just remember, children copy the way they see you dealing with your emotions. If you expect them to be more controlled in their expressions of anger, they must first see it modeled by you.

When emotions are dealt with in the early stages and allowed to be expressed in words, it eliminates the need for those emotions to be acted out in other behavior.

If misbehavior at this emotionally based level is not handled effectively in the early stages, troublesome emotions build and become like giants that eventually control our lives.

Often the unresolved emotions of children become focused against parents and other individuals in authority positions in the form of rebellion or revenge. The child reasons, *If I can't win, at least I can get back at them.* When decisions begin to be made out of rebellion, look out! This is a sign that something is wrong in the parent-child relationship, and if this alienation is allowed to grow, it can cause deep-seated dysfunction.

Unresolved negative emotions tend to grow more and more ugly until they are forced to be acted out in rebellious, antisocial, destructive, revengeful ways. Once this becomes the primary mode of a child's behavior, you, your family, and society are in trouble, and you should probably seek professional help to get to the root of the problem.

One of the most common ways in which children express unresolved emotions is to become covertly revengeful. This is especially true when the parents' only mode of attack is to chip away at the tip of the iceberg behavior they don't like. In other words, children are afraid they'll be punished if they are up-front and tell their folks off, so they become underhanded, getting back at their folks in subtle, passive ways.

Children who refuse to do anything at home may not be lazy, but they may be rebelling in a passive way. The children who behind their parents' back deliberately do what their parents have strictly forbidden may be doing it for revenge. Other children lie or steal or are destructive. Here's an example:

One day I answered the phone, and the frantic mother's first words on the other end of the line were "Don't hang up. If you don't help me I'm going to kill my 3-year-old daughter."

With all the calm I could muster, I asked, "What did your daughter do?"

"She just took a metal nail file and put a scratch all the way around my brand-new baby grand piano."

I could understand why the mother felt the way she did. I asked, "Is that all she has done?"

"No," the mother replied just a little calmer. "Last week I noticed she cut the bottoms off the curtains in my bedroom."

"Is that all?"

"Well, no," she continued. "Ever since the baby was born she has been urinating on the living room carpet, and it's beginning to stink."

What this mother was beginning to weave for me was a tapestry of typical passive-aggressive behavior. This 3-year-old was in rebellion against her mother, probably over some unresolved emotional issues such as jealousy, anger, hostility, or fear of loss of love. What drove the expression of revenge underground was her fear of her parent's harsh punishment. How much better to have allowed the child to talk about troublesome feelings when the first signs of misbehavior surfaced than to have tried to squelch this behavior and then had these feelings seep out in destructive, hostile revenge.

Let's go back for one more lesson from Iceberg Psychology 101. When a piece of the iceberg is chipped away, what happens? The iceberg doesn't just sink deeper into the sea. Rather the iceberg adjusts to the loss by bringing something else to the surface. In human behavior you can get rid of the misbehavior you don't like by chipping away at it until the child is afraid to do it ever again, but that doesn't solve the underlying problem, and it will surface in a slightly different form. And let me warn you, typically the secondary behavior will be worse than the first.

An example is the child who has been threatened with punishment if she ever wakes the sleeping baby. That may be enough to stop the child from waking the baby, but if jealousy is still under the surface, what is there to prevent the child from flushing the baby's teddy bear down the toilet, or scribbling on the walls of the nursery?

Emotionally based misbehavior is not easy for some parents to deal with. Many parents resort, without thinking, to dealing with this behavior the way emotions were handled in their own homes of origin. Perhaps the most dysfunctional way is to block or stuff feelings and refuse to allow a child the verbal expression of such emotions as anger, jealousy, fear, or revenge. I call these unresolved or stuffed emotions "garbage." What do you do with the literal trash or garbage that accumulates in your home? When you get a sack of garbage, do you say, "Oh, how wonderful! I have another sack of garbage," and then place the garbage in the closet that contains your clothing or keepsakes? Of course not. You bag that smelly, rotten stuff up and lug it out to the curb for the garbage truck to carry away and dispose of.

The problem in many families is that parents don't know how to get rid of the emotional garbage in their lives. They bag it up (stuff it) and put it in a closet of their mind where it grows more rancid and smelly and ends up contaminating the rest of their lives. This emotional garbage then affects the way they parent their children, causing their children to begin saving their own bags of garbage to foul up their lives as well.

The stench of old emotional garbage, however, can never be contained, and eventually it spreads beyond parent-child relationships to all the other relationships in the child's life—teachers, peers, employers, scout or church leaders, and eventually government officials.

Back to the literal garbage. When it accumulates, what do you do, again? You bag that garbage up as quickly as you can and drag it out to the curb, where it will be picked up and disposed of. The equivalent of dragging our emotional garbage out to the curb is to get it out of our lives by talking about it, resolving issues as they surface. The Christian will ask God's garbage truck to pick it up and dispose of it!

Disposal starts by admitting an emotion—"I'm angry"—and then focusing on the situation that caused the emotion to see how it can be changed so the emotion does not have to be experienced in the future. The word "when" helps you do that. "I feel angry *when* the kids run through the house screaming." Further clarification can come when you ask why—"*because* I enjoy a peaceful, orderly atmosphere in my home."

This simple technique of admitting an emotion and clarifying the *when* and *why* of it keeps the garbage out of the closet and helps us know how to go about solving the problem that caused the emotion in the first place. "I feel frustrated when you run and scream in the house, because I'm trying to listen to the news."

Your next task is to help your child practice this method of talking through troublesome emotions by being willing to listen and encouraging problem-solving. This way, emotions won't sit around in the closets of his or her life growing more putrid until the child rebels or is motivated by revenge.

Emotions aren't good or bad; they just are. But too much emotion sabotages the process of easy obedience. Therefore, when you see emotionally based misbehavior, think of what you've learned in Iceberg Psychology 101. Instead of chipping away at the tip of the iceberg behavior you don't like, identify the negative emotions under the surface that are causing the problem. Then by talking out the emotion and solving the problem, your child won't have to act it out, and hopefully it will melt away.

Chapter 7

Preparation for Confrontation

The time to start correcting the child is before they start correcting you.—Homer Phillips.

Every B.C. (Before Children) person I've ever met has watched the child in the shopping cart throwing a fit at the checkout stand and said, "My kid will never do that." And all the A.D. (After Delivery) people I have known have had to eat their words. The very nature of children who must grow into healthy, autonomous individuals with the power to think for themselves and make their own choices, means that sooner or later they will be at loggerheads with people who are in authority—who think differently and have the power to enforce their will.

For most families these collisions start around the second birthday. There is a reason this stage is called "the terrible twos." Few parents, even those who are calm, caring, and creative, can escape all power struggles. That's why it's important to prepare early for these confrontations. If you master the next four steps, even though you won't be able to avoid all confrontations you will know what to do to have a more likely chance of both you and your children coming out winners.

Here are the four prerequisites that will help you prepare yourself for the coming conflict:

1. *Temper your temper.* It's natural for children in their attempt to test the results of certain actions or emotional expressions to copy others—especially their parents. Even tiny infants have the uncanny ability to imitate. Just stick out your tongue at a newborn. Keep repeating this action, and chances are the baby will stick out his or her tongue too. Isn't that amazing?

This imitative behavior is one important way that children learn to act properly—or improperly. And since highly emotional behavior, such as aggression, is the easiest modeled behavior, that's all the more reason that your children see you acting calmly and rationally in the face of conflict.

When I was teaching nursery school, I had a 4-year-old boy who behaved very strangely whenever he got angry. I finally confronted his mother. "When Keith is angry, why does he go to the wall or the nearest large object—a table or a chair—and beat on it as if he were a boxer?"

"Oh," replied his mother, beginning to laugh, "that's how his father reacts when he gets angry. Just last night he got angry while we were in the kitchen, and he turned around to the refrigerator and beat on it just like that!"

If children pound their fists on a table, stamp their little feet, and scream, we call it a temper tantrum and do whatever possible to stop the uncontrolled behavior. But adults? Well, most moms and dads tend to get away with it, and for too many a show of temper becomes the only method of getting their children to obey immediately. But because it works does it mean it helps promote those three vital goals of easy obedience—to become self-disciplined, to prevent or resolve conflict, and to preserve or build self-worth? No! The parents end up in control, there's sure to be an even bigger conflict in the future, and it's demeaning.

Children are quick to figure out that even though Mom or Dad may ask a dozen times, they rarely do anything to make sure their children obey until after they get so angry that they end up screaming. The result is that children wait until they hear the screaming before they obey. They know their parents mean business then, and they'd better do what is asked immediately or they'll get it! Because children tend to obey after they've been screamed at, their obedience serves as a reinforcement to their parents' temper tantrums. So Mom and Dad end up pounding the table, stamping their feet, and screaming more often.

It's a vicious and dysfunctional cycle. But it can be broken, and it must be, because the obedience you gain through losing your temper is not as valuable as what you lose. Every time you lose your temper and your children see your uncontrolled behavior, you lose their respect.

Think about it. How much respect would you have for a police officer if he got angry with you, pounded his fists on the hood of your car, stamped his feet, and screamed, "Why are you double parked?"

You might remember not to double park, because you know that if you do you'll get a ticket. But because he lost his temper, your respect for him would be nil. When it comes to parenting, none of us can afford to lose the respect of our children.

There's another reason throwing a temper tantrum (and particularly screaming) is not a good way to get obedience. It destroys self-worth.

How would you feel if someone who was your authority (a teacher or an employer) got angry and screamed at you? You'd probably feel like shriveling up and blowing away. Add an audience, and you'd feel verbally tarred and feathered. Now, you might quickly do what that authority wanted you to do, but you'd despise that person for embarrassing you.

Children are similar to grown-ups in this respect. They don't like being belittled or demeaned, especially in front of an audience.

None of us like to admit that we might, on occasion, get so angry we would impulsively scream at our children. We treasure our children as special gifts of God, and we don't want to intentionally do anything that might be damaging to their self-worth. We certainly don't want anyone else to know that we occasionally lose our cool.

It reminds me of the story I once heard of a little boy asking his mom, "Mommy, why is it that you always quit screaming at me when Daddy comes home?" We don't even want our spouses to know we scream at our children when no one else is around. Instead, we must learn to turn our screaming into singing, and our yelling into yakking. In other words, don't act out your anger. Instead, put it calmly into words. Here are some ideas:

If your child isn't paying attention the first or second time you speak, try lowering your voice instead of raising it. Go over to your child, look him or her in the eyes, and whisper your message. I know teachers who have maintained wonderful control over their classrooms mainly by lowering their voices to a whisper if there was too much noise. The students responded by being more quiet so they could hear.

Or you might want to go one step further and try the silent method. Just go and stand next to your child, perhaps touching the back or an arm. Don't say anything until he or she turns and looks at you. When you have your child's full attention, make your request.

If nothing else works, you could always make your request over the phone, if you have two telephones in the house and a local phone system that allows you to call yourself. Call your own number, hang up, and let it ring. When your child answers, pick up your phone again and you'll have full attention.

Once you have your child's attention, make your request clearly and firmly. Then make sure you follow up so you are certain he or she is doing what you want. When you do this, you'll find a significant increase in your child's compliance without any harmful side effects. And you'll feel a whole lot better by having tempered your temper!

2. *Establish unbendable rules.* Most children grow up with 9,528 rules that cover every minor infraction. But what good are rules if the child can't remember them? If you've ever heard your children complaining, "But Dad, I don't remember you ever telling me that," then chances are you've given them more rules than they can remember. Rules alone don't make well-disciplined children! It's the rule that is enforced consistently that gets obeyed.

It's easy to fall into the trap of having too many rules. Here is how it happens: Babies can't generalize that if touching the knobs on the TV is wrong, so is touching the stereo knobs. They must be carefully taught every specific thing you don't want them to do. You quickly learn to say no to each questionable situation or behavior, since this is the only effective way to teach babies. Without thinking, you continue to make up more and more rules, until you have made so many rules for your children to obey that even you can't remember them all!

If a child tries to operate on rules alone, here is what happens: A questionable situation comes up, and Bette needs to decide what to do. She flips through her mental rulebook. If she can't remember a rule against it, then she decides it must be OK, and she goes ahead and does what she wants. If it turns out to be wrong and her parents ask, "Why did you do it?" the child often blames them. "You never told me not to!" Or if there was an already established rule, she simply says, "I forgot!"

Just making up more rules is never going to help your children learn what is right or wrong. If they are not clear on what makes a behavior right or wrong, then they'll never be able to make wise decisions on their own.

So throw away your rulebook. Instead, establish three basic commandments as the code of behavior for your children—and *you!* Here they are:

1. You may not hurt yourself.
2. You may not hurt others.
3. You may not hurt things.

These three basic principles cover an abundance of misbehavior, allowing the child the necessary framework for making decisions. Without these three rules, kids can make some pretty foolish decisions. For example, Jack wants to play baseball in your front yard. He checks the old rulebook and can't remember whether you have ever said, "No baseball in the front yard." He does recall that rule number 5,422 says, "No football next to the garden." That's similar, but this is the front yard, not the garden, and it's baseball, not football. So he calls "Batter up" without ever thinking about the picture window a few yards away!

But if he would apply the three commandments to this situation, he would ask, "Will playing baseball in the front yard hurt me? No. Will it hurt others? No. Will it hurt things? Uh-oh, there is the picture window. It could easily get broken. I guess I had better not play baseball in the front yard."

Start teaching these unbreakable commandments by tagging them onto more specific limits. You might say, "No playing in the street, because you may not hurt yourself." "I can't let you hit your brother, because you may not hurt others." "No jumping on the beds, because you may not hurt things."

I don't want you to get the idea that these three basic commandments are effective only for the younger set. Not at all. They can continue to be effective throughout the growing years. Here are some examples of things you might tell your teenager:

"No, I can't let you sit out in the car and neck. Emotions can easily get out of hand and lead to a sexual encounter. I don't want you doing anything that might ultimately hurt yourself or someone else."

"You won't be able to go to the game until your homework is done. Grades are important if you want to get that state scholarship, and I can't let you do anything that might hurt yourself."

"John, you'll have to change shoes before playing ball on the lawn.

Cleats are too hard on the new grass, and I can't let you hurt things."

If you are consistent in applying these three commandments to the various limits in your home, it won't take long for your children to get the idea. The more often you remind them of these commandments in the early years, the sooner they will start applying them to the decisions they make about what they should or should not do. And when this happens, you will find your job as the family disciplinarian a whole lot easier.

3. *Categorize your child's behavior.* Many of the confrontations parents have with their children are unnecessary. Too many parents major in the minors when it comes to discipline. They focus on relatively inconsequential behavior that will eventually cease with maturity, when they should be focusing on getting rid of troublesome behavior that if left to grow will ultimately destroy the child's hope for happiness and good family relationships.

You can't teach your child everything at once. If you try, you will be constantly nagging, and the consequence of this is not very pleasant. In the first place, you'll become negative and frustrated and miss the joy of parenting. Second, you'll make your child's life miserable. Most children can take pushy parents only so long before they start rebelling. Some rebel openly by refusing to obey and by acting out their anger in destructive or hurtful ways. Others try to get back at their parents by resorting to passive aggression. In other words, they "win" by doing annoying things behind their parents' back or by just refusing to listen or act on what they say.

But the biggest consequence of trying to teach your child everything at once is that you'll be so busy correcting the minor infractions that you may not have the energy or time to deal with the major ones—the behavior that violates one of the three basic commandments of not hurting yourself, others, or things. If this happens, the child will begin to feel that these rules are really not so important after all, and will lose respect for your authority.

Therefore, you must decide what is really important to you at this time and concentrate on teaching those things. Once those lessons are learned, you can move on to secondary matters. I've found it helps to begin by dividing your child's behavior into three categories:

Category 1, *acceptable behavior*—behavior you approve of and would like to see more often. Your list might include such things as being polite, sharing toys, sorting the dirty clothes, or playing quietly while the baby naps.

Category 2, *unacceptable behavior*—behavior that you can't allow because it breaks one of the three basic commandments of hurting yourself, others, or things. This list might include standing up in the bathtub, biting siblings, or throwing things in the house.

Category 3, *annoying behavior*—behavior that you may not like but that you can live with! This will probably be your longest list. Category 3 behaviors might include such things as making "lumpy" beds, with the sheet hanging below the bedspread; using a thumb to push the last bite on the fork; leaving the bathroom mirror spotted; or showering for 15 minutes when five is sufficient.

Once you have categorized your child's behaviors, then your plan of action is simple.

For category 1, *acceptable behavior:* reward the behavior you approve.

For category 2, *unacceptable behavior:* correct the behavior you can't allow.

For category 3, *annoying behavior:* either ignore the things you may not like but can tolerate, or creatively teach the child more appropriate behavior. The creative discipline techniques in this book are extremely effective when dealing with category 3 behavior.

Your first step in dealing with category 3 behavior is to prioritize these amazing behaviors according to how badly they bother you. You must decide what's really important to deal with *now.* Making the bed may be important, but not as important as brushing teeth and saying please. Therefore, concentrate on brushing teeth and saying please. Once these become habitual, you can move on to teach other behaviors creatively.

Carefully monitor yourself—and your child. If you notice you are correcting more than you are rewarding, something is wrong. Delay trying to change some of those category 3 behaviors and concentrate on what's really important *now.* Don't fall into the trap of being a negative parent. Enjoy yourself. Parenting should be fun!

And watch your children. If you notice a cloud of negativism come over their usually sunny dispositions, and if you begin to detect some subtle resistance to your suggestions, it just may be you're pushing or correcting too much. It's a lot better to back off for a while and reestablish a positive relationship with your children than to push blindly on and take the chance of ending up with rebellious kids sometime in the future.

A mother once wrote, "Our son wanted to get a flattop haircut. I almost fainted. His dad asked, 'How are your grades, son?' He was at the top of his class. So his dad said, 'Then you should be able to make a good decision about what kind of hairstyle you would like to wear.'" Parents who practice easy obedience don't get hung up on category 3 behaviors that if enforced could cause conflict. When it comes to discipline, they keep their priorities straight—rewarding the positive category 1 behaviors and correcting the negative category 2 behaviors.

4. *Determine who owns the problem.* Many parents believe that if they are wise enough, smart enough, and skilled enough, they can pretty well solve their child's behavior problems. That's not really true. Only the person who owns the problem can solve the problem. No matter how many strategies you may use, some problems are beyond your control.

Why? Because there are two kinds of problems children have: situation problems that can be solved by modifying the situation or environment in some way, and person problems that can be solved only when the person with the problem chooses to change.

Most early behavior problems are situation problems. These are problems that can be solved by a situational change. You can ward off the problem by meeting your child's needs before he or she has to misbehave to get your attention. In other cases you take control and through discipline the problem is solved. Here are some common situation problems and their solutions:

Your baby cries. You change the diaper. The crying stops.

Your toddler throws food from the table. Her plate is removed. No more throwing.

Your child is whining. You put the child in bed for a nap. He wakes up happy.

Your kids are throwing their jackets on the floor. You provide a coatrack by the front door. They begin hanging up their jackets.

Joyce experienced a typical situation problem with 4-year-old Betsy. Betsy was making everyone late for school. After breakfast, instead of brushing her teeth and putting on her coat so she was ready to leave, she just dawdled. Mom tried getting her up earlier in the morning, but that didn't seem to help. Even when breakfast was finished ahead of schedule, Betsy still couldn't get ready on time.

Finally, Mom talked to Betsy about the problem and learned that even though Betsy loved kindergarten, she really wanted to spend more time with her mom. By dawdling each morning she was able to get more of her mom's attention, even though it was mostly negative.

Joyce admitted that the morning hours were hectic, and Betsy didn't get much attention unless she misbehaved. So she decided to try an experiment. She made lunches and set the table the night before so she would have an extra 20 minutes in the morning to devote to Betsy. She would read to her, play dolls, or have a tea party—whatever Betsy wanted. The result? Betsy blossomed with this extra attention, and the problem disappeared.

Joyce realized that the problem of not getting ready for school on time was not Betsy's problem per se, but a situational problem brought on by Betsy's need for attention. Joyce's plan of attack, therefore, was to change the situation, and the problem was quickly resolved. If Joyce had misdiagnosed the problem, she would probably have doubled her efforts at correcting and criticizing Betsy and would have unknowingly contributed to the problem.

A grandmother once told me about the difficulty she had keeping her son's shirt tucked in, especially when he went to school. She nagged, threatened, and lectured him about the importance of looking his best, but nothing seemed to work. Finally one day inspiration hit. She ceased mentioning, "Tuck in your shirt." She merely sewed lace on his shirttails. Never again did she have to remind him. Suddenly her son had a reason to do what his mother had asked.

Not all problems are as simple to solve. Sometimes you must change your plan of attack, or you must try a wide variety of solutions before you find one that really works. Often situation problems that could have been solved easily by a change in the environment become deep-seated person problems that affect every aspect of a child's life—such as the habit of showing off in order to get attention, or lying out of fear of harsh punishment. This is behavior you want to prevent.

Some problems are a combination of the two. They may start out as a situation problem but fairly quickly move into the arena of a person problem. This is especially true when problems become habits. For example, have you ever tried to cure a 5-year-old of sucking her thumb? You remind her 386 times a day, put bitter-tasting stuff all over her thumbs, make her wear mittens to bed, and pay the dentist to install an antithumb-sucking device in her mouth. But after all your well-meaning effort, your 5-year-old is still sucking away. Why? Because the problem has become a person problem and is no longer a situation problem.

At birth, thumb sucking might be considered a situation problem. If parents are consistent and persistent enough, the child will often accept a pacifier. If not, thumb sucking quickly becomes a habit—a person problem. And when this happens, the only way the parent-imposed situational reminders can help is if the child wants to stop sucking his or her thumb.

We experienced this with Kari. I tried every known method; we even had a dental appliance with sharp prongs put on her to stop tongue thrusting. It was guaranteed to stop a child from sucking as well, but it didn't. However, once Kari decided she wanted to stop, she asked for help. "Mom, put the yucky stuff on my thumb to help me remember. Can I wear mittens to bed to help me to remember?" No longer did she resent our reminders.

I've learned that the longer inappropriate actions are tolerated, the more they become a part of the child's spontaneous behavior. Once this occurs, then no amount of parental pressure, manipulation, strategy, or punishment will work. Change will come only after the child chooses to change.

It's at this time (when a child wants to change) that a motivational reminder may be most helpful. Motivation is what it took to solve Henry's teasing problem. Henry was a saint with other people, but when he got around his younger brothers and sisters his halo disappeared. He teased them unmercifully. No matter what they said, he would retort with some catty remark. He made everyone in the family miserable. He was no fun to be around.

Mom was beside herself. There must be some way to get Henry to change his snide remarks into kind ones. When Henry was younger, she tried punishing him—sending him to the time-out room every time he teased.

When this didn't work, she made him say three nice things about the person for every awful thing he said. But the tug of war that took place to extract words of kindness and appreciation from Henry was hardly worth it.

Mom tried withholding privileges. Once Henry went without his bike for a month; but no problem—he just took up skateboarding!

As Henry got older, he realized that teasing hurt people's feelings and it wasn't something he wanted to do, but still he couldn't seem to break his teasing habit.

It was then that Mom realized that Henry's problem was indeed Henry's problem. He admitted he wanted to change but couldn't. That's when they came up with the idea of a motivational reminder! Without telling Henry, Mom purchased the baseball mitt Henry had been wanting. She had it wrapped in a beautiful box and tied with a bow. She then took the box home to Henry and told him that there was something in the box that he really wanted, but the only way he could earn the right to open the package was to convince the family that teasing was no longer a part of his behavior.

Mom placed the package on top of the refrigerator, where Henry would be sure to see it every time he walked by.

Henry slipped up a few times, but when he remembered the package, he stopped himself. And his siblings were helpful too. When he would begin to tease, all they had to say was "Henry, remember the package!" and he would apologize.

The last time I talked to Henry's mom, the package had been sitting on the refrigerator for two months! But Henry had made definite improvement, and she was quite hopeful that the family would soon vote to allow Henry to open the package.

Why did the wrapped package work? Henry already knew he should change, and he wanted to, but motivation was lacking. Changing the situation enough so he could see the package on top of the refrigerator every day made him elevate the necessity for change to a top priority.

If you have tried a dozen ways to get your child to stop a negative behavior and nothing works, admit defeat. Chances are the problem is no longer a situation problem. Approach the problem as a person problem and try the following:

1. *Talk to your children about their problems.* Help them recognize the problem as theirs, and point out the negative effect this behavior will have on them unless it is corrected.

2. *Tell your children you are willing to help*—but only if they want to change and seek your help. As with Henry, it just may be that a motivational reminder is all your child needs to give him or her the oomph to overcome that troublesome habit.

3. *Start building your children's self-worth.* Fill their love cups. Encourage. Instead of discipline in the traditional sense, a completely different approach is now needed. Only people with a healthy dose of self-worth have the courage necessary to admit their errors and the ego strength necessary to harness the means to overcome their problems.

Remember, you cannot make your children perfect. Don't feel guilty or embarrassed over behavior you can't control. You do them an injustice if you accept the blame for problems that are really theirs. Instead, help your children to see that they are the builders of their own personalities, characters, and reputations. They can choose the characteristics they want to develop. Sometimes they may feel like the apostle Paul and end up doing what they don't want to do and not doing what they know they should do. But Christ can give them the courage and the self-control necessary to change—if they ask for His help.

If your children have a person problem and want to solve it, encourage them to hold fast to the promise in Mark 10:27: "With God all things are possible."

Chapter 8

Teaching Easy Obedience

One of the hardest jobs for a parent is making a child realize that "no" is a complete sentence.—Author Unknown.

To maintain good rapport with your children doesn't mean you should be indifferent to misbehavior or be afraid to lay down the law if necessary. Quite the opposite. Easy obedience and positive parent-child relationships happen only if parents are strong enough to establish, maintain, and enforce limits. Only then will children feel secure in their environment and respect the adult enough to obey willingly.

When children feel they are the strongest members of the family, it's scary for them. They know they don't have all the answers. Insecure children tend to feel that when they are in control, their environment is predictable and less threatening. Therefore, they try to control the people around them with anger, tantrums, threats, and defiance. You can easily see why parents who are not willing or able to stand up to their convictions and take a proactive role in disciplining their children have kids who are miserable to live with.

Sometimes you have to travel a rocky road for a short time to get to where you want to go. It's the same with discipline. You sometimes have to stand firm in spite of conflict, anger, or resentment in order for your children to realize they can't have their own way. When the obedience lesson is learned, children cease fighting, and you can more quickly get back to smooth relationships based on mutual respect.

Teaching children to obey doesn't have to be a tiresome task. It can be fun. However, you can't laugh, play games, and joke with your children and expect obedience unless you establish certain ground rules or limits—a code of behavior by which they must live.

Obedience is the most important lesson a child must learn—so it's absolutely necessary that you make the lesson easy. Make it enjoyable. Find subtle ways to encourage, influence, and motivate your child to live within the limits. Make it worthwhile for your child to obey. Sure, it's human nature to test the limits occasionally, and kids wouldn't be kids if they didn't. But your goal is to establish within your children a basic willingness to obey. And your success depends on you—their first and most important teacher!

Being a respected authority

An essential factor in teaching children obedience is to establish their respect for your authority by making sure you enforce your requests consistently.

In the early months and years, you must teach your children that "Father or Mother knows best." They must learn to trust you to make wise decisions for them when they are too young or immature to know what's good for themselves. This is the time to establish your credibility as an expert decision-maker, an authority. The longer you wait to teach this lesson, the harder it will be for your child to learn.

For many people the word "authority" conjures up images of judges, rulers, or police officers—those with the power to enforce unpleasant rules and regulations. But an authority is also a specialist, a wise person, an expert. This is the kind of authority you must strive to become as a parent. Your children should obey you because they trust your wisdom and expertise, not because they fear your superior power or strength.

The first few years of your child's life are the time to convey the message of your authority. To do this you must enforce your instructions and requests immediately. However, make sure that your instructions are enforceable. Too many parents go about teaching the obedience lesson in the wrong way, trying to enforce the unenforceable. For example, they say something like this: "Stop crying. Now, I'll have no more of that. If you don't stop crying this instant, I'll give you something to cry about!" Sound familiar? Or this: "Eat those vegetables. I said eat them—don't you dare spit them out."

Parents have also been heard saying such things as "If I've told you once, I've told you a million times, go to sleep!" Or in the struggle of trying to get a child toilet trained, they may demand, "No more wetting your pants. You're a big boy. Use the toilet!"

If you're like most parents, I bet you've gone through hassles such as trying to get your children to stop crying, eat their dinner, go to sleep, or go to the bathroom in the proper place. It's not that these requests are wrong; it's just that they may be given prematurely, before you've taught your child that you are the authority—a respected authority!

Requests concerning a child's body functions can't be enforced. You can shout until you're blue in the face, threaten, and bribe—but if children really don't want to do it, they have ultimate control of their crying, eating, sleeping, and eliminating. Therefore, these requests are almost impossible to enforce. So don't start there. Start with requests that are realistic—requests that you can enforce. For example:

"Come inside." (Go out and bring your child in.)

"Turn off the TV." (Take your little one to the TV and help her turn it off.)

"Don't hit your brother." (Separate them.)

"Wash your face and hands." (Lead your child to the basin and hand him soap and a washcloth.)

"Button your shirt." (Help him button it.)

"Put your bike away." (Take your child by the hand and lead her to the bicycle. Help her put it away.)

When your children have learned to be obedient to the requests that you are able to enforce, then because they respect you, they will be more willing to obey requests that you can't really enforce because of the children's control over their own body functions or emotions.

Once you have decided that you can enforce a certain request, here is the procedure to follow:

Step 1: *Make a request.* Say it once, and be sure that your child hears and understands.

Step 2. *Reward.* If your child responds positively, reward with a word of appreciation at the feeling level ("I'm happy when you do what I ask") or with a special demonstration of love, such as a hug or a smile.

Step 3. *Enforce.* If your child doesn't respond, repeat the request as you begin to enforce it. For example, "I asked you to come into the house for supper." Then do whatever is necessary to get your child's willing compliance. For example, make a game of getting to the house. "I bet I can beat you to the back door!" "Let's guess how many steps it will take to get to your chair at the table!" You might want to take the child's hand and skip to the door.

When you enforce a request or limit, there is no need to be harsh and punitive. Your words and actions should convey two important messages: You expect obedience, and you will interrupt whatever you are doing to enforce your request.

The key to easy obedience is captured in this jingle:

> Tell the child one thing to do,
> and then make sure you follow through.

As children get older and more verbal, beware of distraction techniques that your child may try to use to get out of having to obey, or to delay obedience. "It isn't my turn to empty the trash." "I did it last time." "It isn't fair." Even "I love you, Mommy" or "What time is it?" can be attempts at distraction. Sometimes children's comments or questions are legitimate and you need to supply reasonable information, but bright, verbal children can misuse their right for information, and their arguing becomes a way to forestall the inevitable. Or they may hope their parents just get frustrated and give up trying to enforce the request.

Many parents fall right into the child's trap, and their request gets sidetracked while they engage in trying to convince junior that it is his turn, that the request is fair, or whatever. Others become frustrated, explode, forget everything they learned about easy obedience techniques, and apply parental power to force their child to do what is asked. But there is a better way.

Distraction techniques should be totally ignored—not discussed at all—until the request is obeyed. Here is where you must apply the broken record technique. When junior says, "But Mom-m-m-m-y," take a deep breath, put a smile on your face that says you have the situation well under control, take a step forward, and repeat in a calm, clear manner, "Please take out the trash," "Please make your bed," or whatever the request might be. Then simply repeat your request again after each distraction technique is used. Here's how it might sound.

Mom: "Please empty the trash."
Junior: "It's too hard."
Mom: "Please empty the trash."
Junior: "Why do I have to do it right now?"
Mom: "Please empty the trash."
Junior: "I had to do it last time. You're mean."
Mom: "Please empty the trash."
Junior: "When can I go out to play?"
Mom: "Please empty the trash."

Do you get the idea? You may sound like a broken record, but once your child discovers that distraction techniques don't work, obedience comes much easier.

You must also remember not to hide your request in the middle of irrelevant verbiage. "Danny, please hang up all the clothes that are on your bedroom floor" is much better than "Danny, why are you so sloppy? If I've told you once I've told you a hundred times to pick up the clothes on your bedroom floor. Now do it, and no more dillydallying, or you'll be sorry." It's easy for a request to be lost in the middle of many words.

Finally, never be too busy to teach your child appropriate behavior. Vera was entertaining company. Her 4-year-old son was playing with the kitten in a rough manner. "Sean," his mother said calmly, "pet the kitten gently. Don't pull its tail." Sean acted as if he hadn't heard, and continued mauling the cat. Vera went over to Sean and said, "Sean, I said to pet the kitten gently, and I meant what I said. Please hand me the kitten." At that Sean exploded, threw the kitten across the room, and ran for dear life to his room, thinking he'd be safe there, since Mom was entertaining company and would be too involved to discipline him.

But Vera knew better than to allow such disrespectful behavior to go undisciplined. She excused herself from her guests and explained, "I'm sorry I must leave you alone now, but I must talk to Sean. I don't know how long I will be, but I can't let this behavior go undisciplined." She then left her company, opened Sean's door, and sat down on his bed.

Sean was lying down with his face buried in his pillow. Mom began to rub his back, and for two or three minutes nothing was said. Vera knew that her words would be wasted if Sean's emotions were too strong to allow her to reason with him. Finally Sean could stand the silence no longer. "Did the company leave?"

"No," replied his mom.

"Then what are you doing in here?"

"I can't let you get away with such disrespectful behavior. My most important job is to teach you how to behave appropriately. You are much more important to me than my guests." Then Vera went on to talk to him about how unacceptable his behavior had been. They both decided an appropriate consequence would be for Sean to stay in his room for a while. And if it ever happened again, a spanking would be appropriate, since that would give him some idea of the pain he was causing the kitten.

After about 15 minutes the problem appeared to be settled, and Mom went back to her guests. Surprisingly, they didn't mind her absence. In fact, they respected Vera for putting the training of her child first. But more important, Sean never forgot the fact that his mother, no matter how busy and occupied, was not too busy to discipline him.

It takes time to enforce your requests consistently. But it's worth it, and in the long run it will make obedience easier.

Teaching your child to be obedient to authority is probably the most important lesson of early childhood. By making sure your request has been heard and understood, by rewarding the child for responding positively, and by immediately and consistently enforcing your requests, you should have no trouble teaching your child that you mean what you say.

Remember:

> Just ask your child one thing to do,
> and then make sure you follow through.

This is how you begin teaching easy obedience.

Chapter 9

Setting Obeyable Limits

When Abigail Van Buren was asked if she could give young parents just one word of advice, she replied, "Start early! Be consistent. A child must learn that no means no! It doesn't mean maybe. And maybe doesn't mean yes."

Obedience is the willingness to live within the limits that have been established by others. We find limits on every level of society, and we can quickly get into hot water by ignoring them. The sooner your children can learn the importance of obeying limits, the happier they will be—and the more fulfilling your job as a parent will be. "Children, obey your parents" (Eph. 6:1) is wise counsel. Why is it that some children have such a difficult time obeying?

The best preparation for you in understanding why your child may or may not be obeying is to think carefully about your own attitudes toward limits or laws. Why do you choose to abide by some? Why do you ignore others? Take the speed limit, for example. Every time you drive you must choose whether or not to be obedient. I have a feeling that almost all parents who drive have been guilty of exceeding the limit at one time or another. Many drivers do it daily! What affects your choice? Would you go more than the 65-mile-per-hour speed limit if you knew your car would blow up at 66 mph? None of us would! In fact, most of us wouldn't get near the limit—many of us wouldn't get near the car! The consequence would be too severe.

Now pretend that the only thing that would happen if you exceeded the speed limit would be that a flag would pop out of the hood of your car, announcing to the world, "I'm speeding." And let's say that the only way you could get the flag back down would be to have a police officer give you a ticket and wind it down with a special tool. Would you still go more than 65?

Some might, especially if they were rushing to the hospital or to catch a plane. The consequence would not be that severe. But it would keep most of us on the straight and narrow. We would be embarrassed if other people saw our flag, and since we don't like paying fines, we would choose to stay within the limit.

But what if everyone were driving around with their flags flying? Chances are you would, too. It's very tempting to disregard the limits when everyone else is.

When the speed limit is unclear, it's easy to ignore it or to take our chances of not being caught. In some states there is no consequence until excessive speeds are reached. But traveling through one Eastern state, where the costly consequence for the slightest infraction was clearly posted, I noticed that a lot more drivers were obeying the limit. I was too!

Children react to limits the same way adults do. If the consequence is severe enough to be meaningful, they will be obedient. If they are afraid of the social consequences of disobedience, they will comply. But if the consequence is insignificant and everyone else is ignoring the limits, they will take their chances. And when the limit is unclear—if one thing is stated but there is no consequence for slight infractions, or if there is inconsistent enforcement of the limits—then children will not only bounce up against the limits; more often than not they will bounce right through them.

Here is a checklist of questions to ask yourself to determine the chances of the limit being obeyed:

1. *Do you have your child's attention?* Many sabotage the obedience lesson because they fail to get their child's attention before making the request. Or they try to get attention in such a way as to diminish the likelihood that the child will be psychologically ready for obedience. Let me explain.

Have you ever demanded, "Look at me!" right before you tell the child something that requires obedience? Your motive for saying "Look at me!" is appropriate. You know that your chances for getting obedience are enhanced when you have your child's complete attention before making a request. The problem is that the means you used to get your child's attention does not necessarily accomplish the desired result of obedience. The reason is that "Look at me!" is a demand.

How would you feel if a colleague said "Look at me!" right before asking for something? Chances are you'd resist the request—and if really rebellious, you would even look the other way. None of us like to be pushed around, and demands definitely push us all out of shape.

You can accomplish your desired end without any resistance by merely moving close to your child and placing your hand on the child's back or arm. Most children, unless highly engrossed in some activity, will look up. At that moment smile to reward the child for paying attention, and then make your request.

Perhaps one of the best examples of the effectiveness of this nonevasive method of getting attention can be found in the film about Babe, the pig who acted like a dog that herded sheep. If you've seen the film, you know how resistant the sheep were when the dogs were biting at their hooves and barking, trying to get their attention and obedience. But as soon as Babe said the right password, the sheep immediately looked up and paid attention to the instructions that Babe had for them. Then they willingly obeyed. Of course, the film is fantasy. But if you try a nonoffensive method of getting attention the next time you want your children's obedience, you will find that it works in real life, too.

2. *Is the limit clear?* When you ask your child to mow the lawn, what do you mean? Do you mean that in addition to mowing the lawn, the grass clippings need to be raked into piles and bagged for the trash? Do you also want your child to use the edger? Do you expect the cuttings on the walk to be swept away? If so, be sure to state that exactly.

3. *When do you expect obedience?* Is the time limit clear? Is it reasonable to both you and your child? Does your child agree to this time limit?

"Clean your room" is a common request parents make. But they seldom tell their children how long they have to get it done. By the rate of obedience, you might think some children thought they had about 18 years to accomplish the task! If something needs to be done immediately, let your children know. If appropriate, you might ask when your children think they will be finished, and let them work toward their own goals.

The timing of the request will often determine whether it is obeyable or not. Sometimes parents make requests at inappropriate times, when children are involved in other activities. Setting a time limit that gives some flexibility, or determining with their children the time the request can best be fulfilled, will make the request more palatable than if the parent demands immediate obedience without consideration for their children's personal agenda.

4. *Is the request reasonable?* Children are quick to sense injustice. If a limit seems unfair or they don't understand its importance, they will question and resist unless they are afraid of parental retaliation. If you notice a confused look on your child's face when you make a request, it's good to ask, "Does what I'm asking sound reasonable to you? Do you understand why I've asked you to do this?"

There is always the child who complains, "Why do I have to take out the trash? I'm not planning on being a garbage collector when I'm grown." Or "Why do I need to make my bed? I'll be in it again in eight hours."

Parents sometimes resort to "Because I told you to." That's really not a bad reason. It's OK for parents to ask their children to do things merely because the parent wants them done. But be careful how you say it; use a tone that is not pushy or demanding, which could cause resistance. Instead, say, "I've asked you to do it because I want it done. It may not seem reasonable to you, but it's important to me." For an older child, you could add, "I know in the future you'll want things that won't make sense to me. I hope we have a relationship good enough to respect each other's wants and try to please each other. And right now this is what I want."

5. *Is the consequence for disobedience severe enough to be meaningful?* Have you stated the consequence clearly? Is the consequence logical? Is it tied to the task? Will it teach the lesson you want your children to learn? If you are not yet sure what the consequence should be, have you at least made sure your children know there will be one? Are you prepared to follow through with imposing the consequence? (See chapter 11 for a complete discussion on consequences.)

6. *Is the social pressure such that obedience is possible?* Are other children disobeying the limit, making it more difficult for your child to comply? Negative peer pressure can make obedience extremely difficult at times. On the other hand, is there a possibility for social acceptance if the limit is obeyed or social embarrassment if it is not? Children need approval. Children need positive attention.

7. *Does your child understand your limit?* Can your child tell you in his or her own words what the request is? Have you written it down so it can be read? The more senses children use in learning the limit, the easier it will be for them to be obedient. For example, if they hear it, see what needs to be done, read what you have written down on a list, touch it, or process the request in their own heads and then repeat it, they will more likely remember what you have said and follow through with appropriate obedience.

If you don't want your child bouncing through your limits, then you've got to make it very clear that you mean what you say. Here's how one clever mother taught her child the importance of staying within the limits with a quadruple ice-cream cone.

Mom wanted 4-year-old Terry to clean his room. She knew it was important to make her request very specific so he would know exactly what she was requiring. She also wanted to establish how long he had to get the job done.

So after getting Terry's attention, she said, "Terry, I want you to clean your room. That means make your bed, pick up the blocks on the floor, and put them where they belong on the shelf."

To make sure he was listening she asked him to repeat what she had said. Then she added, "And I will give you exactly one hour to finish the job. That's 60 minutes—not 61. If you are not finished in 60 minutes, there will be a consequence. Do you understand?"

Again Terry repeated what Mom had said and helped set the buzzer that was to ring in 60 minutes. "And Terry," she added, "I'm not going to remind you, as I've done in the past. This time it's up to you to do what I've asked. But remember, if it's not done, there *will* be a consequence."

The clock began ticking. Thirty minutes went by, then 45. Still Terry had not started on his room. As the buzzer was about to ring, Mom realized that Terry wasn't going to make it and that she would have to impose some kind of consequence. She thought of spanking. That would cause pain, but had nothing to do with his ignoring the limits. What about withholding privileges? That didn't seem to fit either. How could she teach him the lesson that she meant what she said?

Suddenly a crazy idea popped into her head. The buzzer rang. Terry had bounced right through the limit. The bed was still unmade, and he hadn't even started picking up the blocks. "Goodbye, Terry," she called. "I'm leaving for the ice-cream shop."

Terry's ears pricked up. "Just a minute," he called, "I'm coming."

"Oh, no, you're not!" Mom said firmly. "You had 60 minutes to clean your room and you didn't do it. So the consequence for not obeying is no ice cream. You have to stay here with Dad."

Terry couldn't believe his mommy would actually go to the ice-cream shop without him. But truth dawned when Mom came home with a quadruple ice-cream cone, sat down in front of Terry, and ate the whole thing herself. (It's amazing to what lengths some parents must go to teach the obedience lesson!)

Do you know what happened the next time Mom said "Clean your room; you have 60 minutes"? Terry had the room spick-and-span in about 10 minutes. And that one time, Mom rewarded Terry by taking him out for ice cream.

It's important not to get into the habit of rewarding children for everything you ask them to do. You must be especially careful about using sweets as a reward. But in this case, it only took one ice-cream cone for Terry to learn the lesson that Mom meant what she said. And learning that you mean what you say is such an important lesson that if it can be taught with one ice-cream cone, then I think it's well worth it. The quadruple ice-cream cone made the lesson of obedience easy and fun. Any time you can do that, you've got a winner!

In summary, here are the parameters that make limits obeyable:

1. Get the child's attention.
2. Make sure the limits are clear.
3. Determine a time limit.
4. Make sure limits are reasonable.
5. Determine a meaningful consequence.
6. Make sure there is positive social influence.
7. Make sure limits are understood.

Chapter 10

The Power of Being Positive

"Children are likely to live up to what you believe of them."—Lady Bird Johnson.

You can follow all the rules for easy obedience and master the techniques but still fall short of your goal because of the emotional atmosphere in your home. Easy obedience is possible only when there is a warm, positive atmosphere and where children are nurtured with positive affirmations and rewarded for positive behavior. The result is children who are generally happy, cheerful, and have a positive outlook toward life. But it all starts with you.

Even if your temperament is not naturally optimistic, you can learn to be a positive parent by mastering two techniques: First, make the yes method of child rearing your goal. Learn to say yes instead of no if at all possible. The second is to follow the 10-to-1 rule—10 positive affirmations to each negative or corrective statement you must make.

The yes method of child rearing

The yes method of child rearing is much more effective than the no method, but it doesn't come naturally. If you have ever said no to your children, only to have them pout, kick, or scream until you ended up saying yes, then you must have realized there has to be a better way. All you have to do the next time your children make a request is to say yes first, unless you really mean no.

The following illustration shows how much more effective the yes method can be. Here's a fast-food restaurant scene that I observed one time:

Mom (to her preschooler): "Eat your burger."
Junior: "I wanna go play on the toys. Can I?"
Mom: "No! Eat your lunch."
Junior (starting to pout): "But I wanna play."
Mom (getting frustrated): "I said, Eat your burger."

Junior (wiggling in his chair and faking a whimper): "I wanna play."

Mom had had it at this point, and turned to her 10-year-old daughter across the table. "Shelly, take off your belt and hand it to me." Mom held the belt in a threatening position while she glared at junior, who was pouting in his chair. Slowly he reached for his burger and took a bite—and Mother turned back to the conversation she was having with a friend.

A few minutes later junior noticed the ice-cream cone his sister had gotten because she finished her meal, and he whined, "I wanna ice cream."

Mom ignored his request and blurted out, "Eat that burger at once, or I'll use this belt."

Junior pouted quietly, then climbed out of his chair and rubbed up against his mother. She reached down, put on his coat, and told his sister, "Take him outside and watch him."

At last the little boy had gotten what he wanted, and he ran happily out to play on the inviting playground equipment. Later he came back in to finish his meal and left with an ice-cream cone!

That's what happens far too often when parents say no. Children have ways of either pouting or nagging their parents into giving in to them. If only this mother had used the yes method of child rearing, what a difference it would have made. For example, the scene could have gone like this:

Mom: "Eat your burger."
Junior: "I wanna go play on the toys. Can I?"
Mom: "Yes, you may go just as soon as you take three more bites."

Junior then bites into the burger and runs happily off to play while Mom eats in peace. We might even pretend that the child runs back indoors and asks, "Mom, will you come and play?" And Mom, using the yes method, might respond, "Yes, after I finish eating. Do you want another bite?" And chances are the child will take a couple more bites before heading back out to the play equipment.

Using the yes method doesn't mean you're wishy-washy, and it doesn't mean you always allow your children to get their way. Everyone wins with the yes method. Just look at the benefits of saying yes: Mother got to eat in peace; junior got to play—and ended up eating just as much as he did with the threat of getting spanked. Sister got to play with a happy sib—and not baby-sit a pouting one. And everyone in the restaurant was able to enjoy their meal.

If the yes method sounds like something you need to cultivate, then start practicing the "yes-but" reply.

"Yes, I know you want to go, but have you considered how you will get your homework done?"

"Yes, you may play outdoors, but you must wear your long underwear, a heavy jacket, boots, and earmuffs, and stay out only 45 minutes."

"Yes, you can have Jill over to play, but you must get your practicing done first."

"Yes, you can go shopping for a new dress, but you'll have to earn the money to pay for it."

"Yes, you may watch the TV program, but you know our family policy about violence. At the first violent act you'll have to turn it off."

Children have the uncanny insight that enables them to recognize when their parents say no but don't really mean it. They then take advantage of this and pout or nag until they get their parents to change their minds. Does this sound familiar?

"Mother, can I have a stick of gum?"

"No."

"Why can't I have a stick of gum?"

"Because I said no."

"But I want a piece of gum."

"I told you, you can't have a stick of gum."

"But I want a piece of gum. I want a stick of gum right now."

"I told you, you cannot have a stick of gum."

"Mommy, Jimmy has a stick of gum."

"I know. It doesn't matter if Jimmy has a stick of gum. I'm not going to give you a stick of gum."

"But Mommy, we've got sugarless gum. Why can't I have a stick of gum?"

"Because I told you, you can't have a stick of gum. Now go out and leave me alone."

"Mommy, why can't I have a stick of gum?"

"Because I'm too busy. I have many things to do, and I'm not going to get up one more time just to get you a stick of gum."

"Mommy, what if I get it myself? Can I have a piece of gum?"

"Oh, OK, you can have a stick of gum. Get it yourself if you want it."

What has happened? The child has won and Mom has lost, big-time—she lost her child's respect because she didn't really mean what she said. But the sad thing is that Mom not only let the child win—she rewarded him for nagging by saying what I call an "idiot no" in the beginning. An idiot no is an impulsive reaction, a no without much thought behind it. Children are quick to discern idiot no's, and they will persist until they find what will turn that idiot no into a yes.

It is a known fact that parents say no to their children's requests much more often than they say yes. Without thinking and for no good reason, the no just tumbles out!

So for the parent who desires easy obedience, here's a good rule to follow: If you don't want your children pouting and nagging you into changing your mind, say no only when you are absolutely sure that you mean no and won't under any circumstances change your mind.

Get into the habit of saying yes. The next time your child says, "May I have dessert?" don't say no; say, "Yes, just as soon as you finish your vegetables." When your child asks in the evening, "May I play outside?" say, "Yes, the first thing in the morning." When your teen wants to use the car, say, "Yes, but it needs to be washed first."

In other words, say yes unless you have a really good reason for saying no and will stick to your decision no matter what. You'll be surprised how often you can say yes to your children without compromising your standards, and how happy your positive response will make them feel. This was demonstrated to me one night when I was trying to put 2-year-old Kevin to bed in his crib. "Mommy sleep with me?" he asked.

Immediately I said no. It seemed impossible. Me in a crib? "I can't," I explained. "I sleep in my own bed with Daddy."

"Please, Mommy, sleep with me," he begged. I continued with my idiot no.

"I'm sorry, Kevin. If I don't sleep with Daddy, he'll be lonesome." (As if Kevin wasn't going to feel lonesome having to sleep alone!)

And to this Kevin replied, "Mommy, you tell Daddy to find another mommy for him so you can sleep with me!"

Well, that was too much. Why not sleep with him for a while? After all, the crib was guaranteed to hold 500 pounds—and Kevin and I together didn't even come close to that! I threw away the idiot no position I had taken and said, "Yes, Kevin, I'll sleep with you for a while—if I don't break your bed!" He giggled as I kicked off my shoes and climbed in, hoping no one would catch me in his crib. Sure, I felt foolish, but Kevin felt like a king!

He snuggled up, and immediately his tense little body relaxed. I whispered a story to him about a little boy I once knew who acted very much like someone Kevin was well acquainted with. And before too long he caught on and shouted, "That's me!" Then after a hug, an Eskimo kiss (rubbing noses), and a butterfly kiss or two, in which I fluttered my eyelash against his cheek, I said good night and climbed out of his crib. Minutes later Kevin was in dreamland. I've always been glad I recognized my idiot no when I did and said yes to Kevin's request. It made him a very happy little boy.

Saying yes to your children is an important way to maintain a positive atmosphere in your home, but there is another equally important way: you must catch your children being good. You can do this if you follow the 10-to-1 rule.

The 10-to-1 rule

Children need positive attention. Criticism, complaining, and negative comments are discouraging and often result in more misbehavior. But encouragement, optimism, and positive strokes are to kids as fertilizer is to plants. It's the stuff that really makes them flourish—remember Rudolf Dreikurs' statement that "each child needs continuous encouragement just as a plant needs water"?

Behavior that gets your attention is rewarded and reinforced. It's easy to notice the misbehavior, but if you want easy obedience you must be careful not to reward that behavior with undue attention. Instead, why not reward the positive? Catch your children in the act of being good. To do this I recommend the 10-to-1 rule: 10 positive strokes to every negative one! Applying this rule will help you become the positive parent you've always wanted to be.

Marcia had always admired positive people. When she was in college, she had the opportunity to spend a summer with a couple who had two young children. For three months she never heard that mom and dad raise their voices to the children. And she determined that someday she wanted to be that kind of parent.

But nine years later, with 4-year-old twin boys racing around the house, her dream of being a positive parent was pretty much shattered. She really hadn't realized just how negative she had become, however, until she decided to record an hour of her interactions with the children. Her purpose was to play the recording back so her boys could listen to it and discuss their negative behavior. But when she began to listen to the tape, the finger of guilt pointed to her. She heard herself saying: "Stop that." "Don't touch the stereo." "No, you can't have it now; I'm busy." "Bryan, if you do that again, you're going to get it." "Brent, no more sassing." "No." "Don't." "Stop!"

She couldn't believe how negative she had become. What had happened to her dream of being a positive parent? She knew children thrived on encouragement, words of appreciation, and positive strokes. Yet during that hour she had recorded, she found herself dealing out 10 negatives to every positive. She immediately determined to turn herself around. Her new goal was to give 10 positives for every negative and see what a difference it made in her children's behavior.

It wasn't an easy assignment. The first thing Marcia began to work on was making requests in a positive way rather than a negative one. Instead of "Don't stand on the table," she said, "Jump to the floor." Instead of "Don't touch the stereo," she said, "I was listening to the music on that station. Please try to find it again for me."

To her surprise, her boys became more compliant. She began to realize that the don'ts she had been giving her children never told them what to do. Making the request positive gave the children guidelines—a direction in which to move.

The second thing she began to change was her response to her children's requests. It seemed that no matter what they asked, she found herself, without thinking, saying no. Now she began a more positive approach. When they asked for a cookie between meals, instead of saying no she would say, "Cookies are for dessert. I have saved this special one for you." If they wanted to watch TV and nothing appropriate was on, she would say, "Let's get the TV schedule and figure out a time when a program is on that you would like to watch." Then she would put forth extra effort to get the boys involved with another activity to take their minds off the TV.

Of course, Marcia found it impossible to be positive all the time. There were still times when a firm no needed to be said. Inappropriate behavior had to be corrected. And occasionally, when she was tired and frustrated, she found herself handing out negative strokes in the form of criticism and threats. But when this happened, she renewed her determination to use the 10-to-1 rule—10 positive strokes for every negative one.

Applying the 10-to-1 rule meant that every time Marcia handed out a negative stroke she had to really look for the positives. She began to notice the little things the boys did that she approved of, and she let them know in the form of a compliment or just a hug or a wink.

It didn't take long for this positive treatment to have an effect on the family. The boys seemed happier. Instead of being bent on persecuting her, they were eager to please. Life was not always a bed of roses, but it was a lot more fun than it had been in the past.

The lack of positive attention can cause tremendous behavior problems in children. For example, one mother complained, "I'm having real problems with my 5-year-old son, Kurt. He is sassy and willful. Whatever I ask him to do, he does the opposite. I can't understand this, since his older brother, Dean, is such a jewel. I try to treat them the same, but I find myself spending more time with Dean because he is such a pleasant person. Why is there such a difference in their behavior?"

It's really surprising, isn't it, when one child is so good and the next so "bad"? Even though you treat both of them the same, you seem to get opposite results. The reason for this is that children are born with different characteristics that may make them either easy or difficult to live with. But regardless of their inborn characteristics, all children need positive attention. They need to feel special. They need to hear compliments and receive recognition. As the eighteenth-century British writer Mary Lamb said: "A child is fed with milk and praise."

When one child in the family is supercompliant and naturally receives abundant amounts of positive attention, the more difficult child notices, at least on an unconscious level. It's interesting how often it is the firstborn who seems to go along with what the parents say, and the second who rebels. The younger begins to feel that the older child (or the submissive child) has a monopoly on getting attention for compliance. The second child reasons that he or she could not possibly be as good, no matter how hard he or she tries, so why compete?

But the difficult child needs and craves attention, and so chooses another area in which to excel—often opting for the role of the rebel. This child would rather have negative attention than little or none.

Chances are this need for attention was what was causing Kurt to be so obnoxious. The question is How can you modify the behavior of a child like Kurt? Here are some ideas:

1. Make sure that both children have their share of positive recognition. This may mean noticing a lot more of the positive things that Kurt does, things that to you may seem insignificant. Reward him for little bits of compliance.

2. Make it fun and easy for Kurt to obey. For a while don't ask him to

do things when you know he will resist. You want as much compliance as possible so you can give more positive attention.

3. Be firm on the limits that are absolutely essential. Don't accept disrespectful or sassy behavior—but don't give him a lot of negative attention for this, either. When it happens, calmly say, "It hurts me when you treat me like that, and you may not hurt others." And then you can send him to his room until he chooses to act appropriately, or impose some other type of discipline.

4. Finally, follow the 10-to-1 rule that Marcia decided to follow. Try to give your child 10 positive strokes to every negative one. Because the more difficult child is obviously going to get a few more negative strokes, you must proportionally increase the positive interactions with that child in order for them to have the same effect. For example, you might notice Kurt's smile, his remembering to say please and thank you, or just his willingness to spend a few extra minutes playing with the dog that doesn't get much attention. You've got to become a master at catching your child being good.

Remember, a positive stroke doesn't always have to be given in words. Smile, wink, ruffle their hair—and your children will get the message that you're tuned in to them and you will be filling their love cups. It can be quite a challenge; but it is worth it.

If you think your children deserve a more positive parent and could use more of your positive attention, why don't you do what Marcia did—and what Kurt's mom decided to do? Record an hour or so of your interactions with your children. If you are leaning toward the negative, I would challenge you to apply the 10-to-1 rule in your family. Ten positives to every negative. And I guarantee that your children will blossom under this positive "rule," and you'll all enjoy life together a whole lot more!

Chapter 11

Let Children Live With the Consequences

The best way to make life hard for your children is to make it too soft for them.—Author Unknown.

Billy goofed around after school and arrived home late. He missed going to the basketball game with his friends—they just couldn't wait.

Sue planted a garden for her school project and forgot to water it. Everything died, and she received an F on the project.

Jim left his good mitt out on the lawn overnight. The automatic sprinkler system came on, and by morning the mitt was a soggy mess. Because the mitt he had to borrow wasn't familiar, Jim missed a fly ball to left field in the championship game that afternoon, and the other team won.

And Terry didn't clean his room in the allotted 60 minutes, so he couldn't go out for ice cream with Mom.

Consequences. They often seem so harsh. Why didn't Billy's mom try to find him after school so he could see his favorite team play? Why didn't Dad water Sue's garden when he saw the radishes drooping? Why didn't Jim's parents remind him to bring in his mitt? It was an expensive loss.

Why? Because these parents had wisely learned that one of the best techniques for modifying children's behavior is to let them suffer the consequences of their inappropriate behavior—to learn from their mistakes. Consequences are especially effective when milder measures, such as reminding or warning a child, have failed to produce behavior changes. Letting a child suffer the consequences is the quickest and, in the long run, the most painless way to encourage a child to make wise decisions.

If children don't understand the link between their actions and certain consequences, they may feel they can get by with whatever they choose. Delinquents, for example, are sometimes surprised when their unlawful behavior finally results in a prison sentence.

"Why me?" they question.

"Why? Because you broke the law!"

"Sure, I broke the law. I've been breaking laws all my life and nothing has ever happened before. Why now?"

It seems incredible that kids think they can disobey certain laws and never have to pay the consequences. But just ask teenagers in trouble, and in most cases you will find that they thought they could get by with it, probably because they always had before.

The only way children are ever going to feel responsible for their behavior is to allow them to suffer the consequences, no matter how painful it may sometimes be to both parents and children. If parents keep bailing them out of the little messes they get themselves into, chances are they'll think they can get out of the big ones, too. And they never will learn responsibility.

Types of consequences

Consequences come in two types: Natural ones and those that are imposed by parents or some other authority figure.

Natural consequences happen automatically if children continue on their own path of "destruction." For example, the natural consequence of eating green apples might be a stomachache; the natural consequence of leaving a room messy might be embarrassment when a teacher comes to visit. Children often learn they'd better not hit others by suffering the natural consequence of getting hit back. Others learn to lock up their bikes, because earlier they didn't, and their bikes were stolen.

Sometimes a natural consequence can be harmful to children, such as the consequence of being hit by a car when playing in the street, or getting burned when experimenting with matches. Parents need to protect children from these terrible consequences, but at the same time teach them to be responsible for their behavior.

Other actions (such as not cleaning one's room) don't carry many natural consequences, so parents have to create one. The way you do this is by imposing a consequence on the child—a logical one, so the child gets the message that the punishment is related to the crime.

Some parents find it hard to impose consequences on their children, and therefore children are seemingly "getting away with murder." And their parents end up being the ones who suffer from their children's irresponsibility!

I once read a story to my children that made a deep impression on me. It was about a poor boy and his mother. One day the boy came home with an egg. When his mother asked him where he got it, he honestly said he took it from under the neighbor's chicken. "You mean you stole it?" his mother questioned.

"Not really," the boy reasoned. "I found it, so I figured it was mine."

His mother didn't like the idea of her son taking the egg, but since he was hungry, she figured one time wouldn't hurt. So she cooked the egg for his supper and told him never to do it again. Do you think this stopped the stealing? Of course not. It just encouraged it. Because he was poor, he felt the world owed him nice things, so he took what he wanted. In the end he was imprisoned for embezzlement. Was he sorry? He was sorry he got caught, but not sorry for stealing. He took no responsibility for his actions. Instead, he blamed his mother: "If stealing was so wrong, why didn't you make me return that first egg I stole—and punish me for it?"

If only this mother had imposed the logical consequence and made her son take back the egg. The brief moment of embarrassment it may have caused her son might have saved him from a life of crime and years of punishment. Parents do not want that to happen to their children. That's why it's so important to link their behavior to consequences. Encourage your children as early as possible to take responsibility for their behavior so they won't have to suffer for it later.

Natural consequences

Being an effective disciplinarian doesn't mean that you always have to be doling out punishment and choice words of wisdom. I've found that some of the biggest lessons my children have learned were lessons they taught themselves by suffering from the natural consequences of their behavior.

For example, one time when Kim, Kari, and Kevin were preschoolers they decided to buy their daddy a box of his favorite candy for his birthday. As soon as the decision was made, they were so excited about getting the candy that they wanted to go shopping immediately. So I drove them to the store. They found the candy box on the shelf and gently carried it to the checkout clerk and started shaking their pennies out of their piggy bank.

At last the candy was purchased, and we headed home. I didn't have time to immediately wrap the gift, so I put it on the top shelf of the pantry, thinking it would be safe there.

But the children had seen where I put it. Later that afternoon one of them said, "Boy, I bet Daddy's candy is delicious. I wish I could have a piece."

"Me too," they all agreed. "I bet Daddy wouldn't even know if we took one piece."

So Kim climbed up on the tall stool and reached for the box of candy. She took out one piece, took off the gold foil, took a bite, and started to hand what was left to Kari.

"No," said Kari, "I want my own piece."

"Me too," chimed in Kevin. So Kim took out two more pieces and gave them to Kari and Kevin. She looked at the box and decided no one could tell any candy was missing, so she put it back on the top shelf.

But the next day they again remembered the candy—and back they went for more. Kim dished out three more pieces. They kept doing this until the box was empty. But they never said anything to me. So the day of Jan's birthday I took the box down and wrapped it. It felt lighter than usual, but I had no idea what the children had done.

"What's in Daddy's package?" the kids asked when they saw the present.

"The candy you bought for Daddy's birthday," I answered.

"But," they gasped, "we can't give Daddy that."

"Why not?" I asked.

"Because it's empty."

"It's empty?" I exclaimed.

"Yes," said the children. "We ate it all up. We'll have to get Daddy some more."

"There isn't time," I explained. "And you don't have any more money. You'll just have to give Daddy an empty birthday present!"

And that's what happened. Jan unwrapped the gift and asked, "What is it?"

"It's an empty birthday present." They hung their heads in embarrassment. "We ate it all up. But we're sorry—and we'll never give you an empty birthday present again!"

They never did!

I could have lectured them about not stealing and about how terrible it was not to have a present for Daddy. I could have sent them to their rooms, or even spanked them. And then, having punished them for their wrongdoing, I could have gone to the store and bought another box of candy. But the effect would never have been the same.

Sometimes it's difficult to allow your child to experience the natural consequence, because good parents want the best for their children. I know one mom who gets up early each day to make a lunch for her teenage boy, even though she said it's his job to make his own. Why? Because she doesn't want him to go hungry. He's not about to put himself out making a lunch when his mom always bails him out. So what should be his responsibility has become hers, because she isn't willing to allow him to suffer the consequence of being hungry.

Another mother takes her child to school when his dawdling causes him to miss the school bus. She doesn't want him to be late. Being tardy would reflect on his citizenship grade, and the teachers might question her competence as a mother if she doesn't care enough about her child to get him to school on time. Consequently, junior misses the school bus more than he makes it. Since Mom is willing to take him, he doesn't need to be responsible.

But good parents don't just put on a good front. Good parents must sometimes swallow their own sensitivity and pride to allow their children to suffer from their irresponsibility for their own good! This is very hard to do. I know.

I finally decided that the problem of getting Kevin dressed in the morning could be solved only if I was willing for him to wear pajamas to nursery school, if that was what he chose to do. I needed to teach him the lesson that it was his responsibility to get dressed.

One day everyone was dressed and ready for breakfast—everyone, that is, except Kevin.

"Kevin, why aren't you dressed?"

"Because," said Kevin, "I was too busy."

"Too busy playing?" asked his dad.

"Oh, no, Daddy, too busy building houses and roads with my blocks."

"But Kevin, your job is to get dressed the first thing in the morning before you eat. The rule is you can't eat breakfast in pajamas," I added.

"But I'm hungry. Can't I eat in pajamas just once? Please?"

I thought about it for a moment. Breakfast was on the table, and we were all sitting down ready to eat, so I suggested that the family vote on it. Everyone raised their hands in favor of it—Kevin raised both of his—and he sat down in his pajamas to eat.

After breakfast everyone scattered to do their last-minute chores. Kevin went into his bedroom to get dressed—but he didn't.

A few minutes later I called, "Kevin, it's almost time to leave for nursery school. You had better get dressed. I'm not going to tell you again."

"OK," said Kevin as he raced his car along the block road and over the bridge, and made a screeching stop next to his block house. Then he noticed the house needed a roof and a garage. He was still working on that task when Jan gave the final call: "Get into the car. It's time for school."

"But I'm not dressed!" said Kevin.

"That's too bad," I said. "You will just have to go to nursery school in your pajamas."

"But my friends will laugh at me!"

"Then get your clothes quickly. You will have to get dressed in the car. We are leaving right now!" I said as I headed for the door.

Kevin grabbed some clothes and raced for the car. It was a short ride to nursery school, so Kevin dressed quickly. Off came his pajamas; on went his underpants; on went the blue shirt. He buttoned it as fast as he could. When he finished there was one extra button at the top and one extra buttonhole at the bottom.

Then he put on the old, torn, green pants and one brown sock. Where was the other sock? He searched the car. No sock. He must have dropped it. What should he do?

"Well," said Kim, trying to be helpful, "one sock is better than no socks."

It wasn't easy for me to let him go to school in that condition. He looked like a neglected child. But the lesson he learned was worth it.

When there is no natural consequence, or the natural consequence is harmful, parents must impose a consequence that will help their children see the folly of their behavior and learn appropriate lessons. You can't allow a 2-year-old to run out into the street. The natural consequence is that the child might get killed. You can't allow a 10-year-old to pick your neighbor's apples without asking. That would be stealing. The neighbor might verbally rip the child apart or send for the police. To allow the child to get away with the theft might encourage this behavior in the future.

Parent-imposed logical consequences

In disciplinary cases in which there is no natural consequence or the natural consequence would be too severe, you must teach children what is inappropriate by using a parent-imposed logical consequence. For example: "If you can't stay out of the street, you'll have to play in the fenced backyard." "If you pick our neighbor's apples, I will have to take $10 from your allowance, and together we will tell Mr. Johnson that this money is your payment for the apples."

Imposing a logical consequence can teach a child a lifetime lesson. For example, Gordon never forgot the time his father took away his car. When Gordon got his driver's license, he and Dad had agreed that if Gordon did not abide by the driving policies that they had decided upon, he would lose the privilege of driving for 30 days. One rule was not to drive out of town without first asking.

One day when Dad was doing business in a nearby town, he was surprised to see Gordon drive down the street with a carful of teenagers. No one had granted him permission. When Gordon returned home, Dad put Gordon's car in the garage, jacked it up, removed all four wheels, and padlocked them together around a telephone pole behind the garage.

Needless to say, Gordon had quite a shock when he discovered it. His dad told him matter-of-factly why the wheels were locked up and said Gordon could have the key to unlock the wheels after 30 days, as they had agreed.

"But Dad," Gordon lamented, "the prom's in two weeks."

"Don't worry," said Dad nonchalantly. "I'll be happy to drive you and your date to the prom."

Gordon learned that when Dad said something, he meant it. And as far as Dad knows, his son never again ignored a rule that carried a consequence.

Some parents say, "I use parent-imposed consequences all the time. If my daughter breaks a window, I spank her. If my son gets into a fight, I spank him. If my child spills some milk, I spank my child." These are parent-imposed consequences, but they are *not* logical consequences that are related to a child's specific behavior.

To be most effective, a parent-imposed consequence must be clearly linked to a child's behavior. When children break a window, they can clean up the mess (if they are old enough not to cut themselves), apologize to the owner, and pay for the damages. If a child gets into a fight with a sibling, a logical consequence might be to be separated or to sit in talk-it-over chairs (two facing chairs) until they have settled their dispute. Even a young child can wipe up spilled milk and learn a lesson about the consequences of carelessness.

The beauty of using natural and logical consequences is that children can never truthfully shout, "Unfair." They begin to learn that the discipline fits the act, and that they deserve to suffer the consequences.

Guidelines for consequences

If you agree with the concept of making your children's "punishments" fit their "crimes," then you'll want to make sure you follow these guidelines:

1. Don't shield your children from consequences that in the long run would be beneficial to them.

2. Don't allow your children to blame others for the predicaments they get themselves into. Neither should you pile blame on your children. It is enough that they are suffering from the consequences of their actions.

3. If the natural consequence is too harmful, or if there is no immediate consequence, impose a logical consequence that is linked to their unacceptable behavior.

4. Support your children in accepting a consequence as beneficial experience. Encourage them to keep a positive attitude about the experience. Help them develop the attitude that a valuable lesson can be learned from each mistake.

5. Don't let your children face major or traumatic consequences without your support. A story I once heard made a tremendous impression on me. The father had said that if the son didn't obey, he would have to sleep in the attic. When the son disobeyed, Father imposed the consequence. But soon after his son went to bed in the attic, the father went up and slept beside him so the child wouldn't be frightened or lonely. When the consequence is a tough one to bear, stay close, if possible, and let your children know that you care. Otherwise, they may become discouraged, and discouragement leads to misbehavior.

6. Decide in advance what logical consequences you would impose on your children for the following acts:

Screaming and yelling when asked to be quiet.
Breaking a toy through carelessness.
Eating a candy bar before lunch.
Playing with matches.
Scribbling on the wall.
Hammering dents in the table.
Telling a lie.
Being disrespectful to an adult.
Forgetting to notify you when they will be late.
Going someplace without permission.

Please stop right here unless you have already done as I suggested and thought of a logical consequence for each of the above. If you didn't, take a second look at the list. It's easier to think of a logical consequence for some kinds of misbehavior than for others, isn't it? For example, if your child screams after you say "Be quiet," you can remove the child from your hearing. For breaking a toy—well, the child has to do without, or maybe pay to get it fixed. Eating a candy bar before lunch might mean no dessert. Matches aren't playthings, and should be taken away and hidden. If children scribble on the wall, they clean the wall; and for hammering on the table, the hammer is taken away.

You may have to think for a while about an appropriate consequence for forgetting to notify you when they'll be late, or for going someplace without permission. Maybe losing the privilege of going someplace special might fit. A consequence for being disrespectful may be separation from the adult by being sent to a time-out room.

But what consequence fits telling a lie? Here you may have to look for a consequence that is associated with the content of the lie. For example, if the child lies about raiding the cookie jar, maybe he or she shouldn't get a cookie the next time they are served for dessert. If children watch TV and then lie about it, perhaps they shouldn't be allowed to watch TV for a while!

Just remember, although it's not always easy to think of a logical consequence, the closer the consequence is to fitting the crime, the more effective it is likely to be!

Self-imposed consequences

It doesn't take much experience for children to have a pretty good idea about what would be a fair consequence for their misbehavior. So if you're in question about what to do, or if your child is older and you feel he or she may resent your discipline, treat a child as God treated King David—allow the child to choose the consequences. God told David not to take a census of the people, but David wanted to know how great his kingdom was, so he went against God's instructions. To teach David the importance of obedience, God gave David the choice of consequences—three years of famine, three months of pursuit in battle, or three days of a fatal plague in the land (see 1 Chron. 21).

Self-imposed consequences are always easier to bear because they are something the person chooses. They can teach a lesson, nevertheless. Here's an illustration:

After Kent had been caught whittling holes in his desk, the teacher asked that he talk to his parents about what should be done. Rather than face them, Kent lied to his teacher, saying he had talked to his parents and they were too busy to fix the desk. Later his parents learned of the situation. After they talked with Kent about it, they decided that in addition to the logical consequence of fixing the desk, the lesson of truthfulness should be emphasized by an immediate consequence for lying. Kent was allowed to choose one of three consequences: not play games with the family that day, forfeit his night out with Dad, or work for two hours weeding the garden. He chose the two-hour weeding job.

Rather than risk your children's resentment of what they consider unjust discipline, allow them to choose, even if you feel their choice may be too lenient. If the lesson is learned, the severity of the consequence doesn't matter. Most parents feel discipline has to be painful—if you make it unpleasant enough, children will never forget the lessons you wanted them to learn. But that's not necessarily so. One mother told me a story about how a sugar cube taught her daughter a lesson that lasted a lifetime—and I think it's worth sharing.

Janine had been grumpy all day. Nothing had gone right. She complained about having to get up. She complained about having to set the table for breakfast. And "Yucky oatmeal again?"

Halfway through the morning, Mom asked, "Janine, can you help me empty the wastebaskets?"

Janine didn't budge. "I'm busy!" she said, not even looking up. Mom continued her cleaning and a few minutes later said, "Janine, I put all the wastebaskets in the hall. Please, can you empty them now so I can get the bedrooms finished?"

"I told you, I'm busy!" Janine responded in an irritated voice.

After lunch Mom asked Janine if she could clear the dishes away. Janine acted as if she'd been asked to move the Empire State Building. "I don't want to do it. It's too much work. I don't feel like working. This is my vacation. I shouldn't have to work."

And that's the way the day went until about 5:00, when Mom asked Janine if she would pick things up before Dad got home. At that simple request, Janine blew up. "Who was your slave last year? Work, work, work. All you do is nag—do this, do that. I can't stand it anymore." Janine turned around and stomped off to her room.

Mom knew that something had to be done, but what? What type of discipline could be strong enough to bring results? Mom gave Janine a few minutes to cool down and then knocked on her door. "Janine, may I come in?"

"Yes," Janine sighed. "Come in."

Mom whispered a prayer, took a deep breath, and began her speech. "Janine, honey, we can't have this behavior anymore. You've been grumpy and negative all day. And you may not sass me! What do I need to do to teach you a lesson that you can't be so sour? I'll let you decide, but remember, it must be something strong enough so that this will never happen again. What do you think I should do?"

Janine thought a few minutes and said, "Give me a sugar cube." Janine's mother had been given a box of fancy, decorated sugar cubes that were used to sweeten coffee or tea.

"A sugar cube?" That certainly wasn't what Mother had in mind as discipline. "Why a sugar cube?"

"Because," said Janine, "I've been so sour. It will remind me to be sweet!"

"Are you sure it will work?" questioned a very doubtful mother.

"Yes, I'm sure," said Janine.

So Mom gave her a sugar cube—and it worked! Whenever Janine was tempted to be sassy and negative, Mom just asked her if she needed another sugar cube, and that's all it took to turn the sour to the sweet.

Isn't that what discipline's all about—teaching a lesson that will last a lifetime? If a sugar cube will do it, why not? Creative disciplinarians don't just haul off and hit a child. They consider carefully the type of discipline that will teach the child the lifetime lesson that obedience pays. So why not make your "punishment" fit the "crime," and start allowing your children to learn from consequences?

Chapter 12

Time-out for Behavior Modification

If you bungle raising your children, I don't think whatever else you do well matters very much.—Jacqueline Kennedy Onassis.

The time-out method of behavior modification is a practical way of imposing consequences. It works successfully on children of all ages, but is especially effective with younger children. It may sound pretty sophisticated, but it isn't. It's really a simple way to reinforce certain behaviors you like and get rid of the ones you don't, without punishing your child. The basic idea is to praise the positive (because when behavior is rewarded it will occur more often) and purposely ignore the negative (because you don't want the negative to be rewarded by your attention).

This method of discipline should start at birth, because it doesn't require language or the child's understanding. Babies just naturally respond to attention, and when they get it for a certain behavior, they tend to repeat that behavior more often. The opposite is also true—behavior that is not rewarded will become less frequent. When I think of the admonition to "train up a child in the way he should go" (Prov. 22:6), I immediately think of rewarding the positive and not the negative. Of all the disciplinary methods, this is the one that requires the closest, most consistent nonpunitive parental involvement with a child.

Problems develop in young children because parents too often reward negative behavior with their undue attention. Later, when the frequency of this behavior becomes problematic, parents resort to punitive methods to extinguish it, causing pain to both parent and child! All this could be prevented if parents would just consistently reward acceptable behavior and not give undue attention to the negative.

As infants become toddlers, it is easier to ignore the negative by having children go to a time-out room or chair, where they are denied any attention. This time-out method of behavior modification is one of the most effective methods you can use for encouraging your child to make long-term behavior changes. But it's not a method that works instantly.

To discourage unacceptable behavior, especially with young children, here is what I suggest: When your child misbehaves, send him or her to a designated room, area, or chair for a short period of time—not more than five minutes. The amount of time spent in the room or in a chair is not the significant factor. The time-out area works because the child is denied your attention for a period of time, and thus is not rewarded for the misbehavior. To use this technique effectively, parents must let their children know that they expect their children's attitude and behavior to be changed when they come out of the room or off the time-out chair, or they are destined to return.

This method of teaching appropriate behavior should not be considered punishment; it is merely a consequence of misbehaving. Your children will accept it without resentment if you carry it out matter-of-factly, without undue force or anger. You can successfully use the time-out technique with your child if you follow these guidelines:

1. Choose *one* behavior that you would like to modify.
2. Count the number of times this behavior occurs during a particular time period—one hour, an afternoon, an entire day. It is best if you do this for three different periods and obtain an average.
3. When your child misbehaves, calmly say, "Time-out for (give reason)," and take the child to the room or chair you have selected. Be sure to tell your child how long the time-out period will be, or allow your child to make that decision by saying "You may come out when you are ready to change your behavior." A general rule to follow with young children is one minute of time-out for each year of age.
4. When your child emerges and acts appropriately, it is most important that you give him or her some time and attention.

My friend Mary tried this technique when she couldn't get her 4-year-old son, Robert, to stop hitting his younger siblings and his playmates. He hit so often that Mary was losing her friends, because their children were afraid to play with Robert. Mary didn't really want to hit Robert for hitting others; that just didn't seem quite right. The last thing Robert needed was the example of his mother hitting!

I told Mary about the time-out method. I explained to her that behavior that is rewarded is reinforced and strengthened. So by getting angry and spending a lot of time punishing a child when he does something wrong puts a lot of emphasis on the misbehavior. It may have just the opposite effect from what you want.

Instead, with no show of emotion, simply say, "Four minutes' time-out for hitting," and take the child to the designated area. Remember, this is not "punishment," so the child can play or do whatever he wants while he's in the room, as long as it's not destructive. The time-out area is merely a place where the child can be so he is not rewarded by your attention. After the allotted time period, allow your child to come out. Don't mention the previous wrongdoing or lecture the child on appropriate behavior. Rather, wait until the child is involved in something you approve of, then spend some time together or give him a word of encouragement or a hug. But the next time the same wrong act occurs, back into the time-out room your child goes.

I asked Mary to count how many times per day Robert was hitting so she would know if the method was being effective. Before trying the time-out method she counted for three days the number of times per day he was hitting. Thirty-three times per day. No wonder it was a problem.

But as soon as she began the time-out method, each day got better until after three weeks he was down to only two or three times per day, and that was something the family could live with.

Mary was so excited about this miracle method that she decided to try it on her 2-year-old daughter, Lisa, who was climbing on the kitchen counters 17 times per day. Seventeen times per day Mom lifted her off the counter and took her to the time-out room. But the result didn't seem to be the same. Two weeks went by without any change.

Then one day, shortly after three weeks of this approach, Lisa stopped climbing on the counters. It was just as if she said to herself, "Well, I guess if I don't want to grow up in the time-out room I'm going to have to give up climbing on counters."

The secret to being successful with the time-out method of behavior modification is persistence. It's a long, slow method of changing behavior, but it's effective if you're there every time the misbehavior occurs and if you do something about it. You can't be inconsistent and expect this method to work.

So if your child has a persistent habit that needs changing, and other methods of discipline just haven't seemed to work, try a time-out period. After three weeks or so of calm, consistent discipline, that habit may just disappear forever.

Behavior modification, as a method of discipline, is based on the principle that problem children act the way they do, not because they were born that way, but because they have learned (you might say they were taught) to behave that way through the rewards or reinforcement they were given. These rewards may have been something positive, such as a piece of candy or hugs and kisses, or something negative, such as a spanking. A spanking is a reward if children want attention and if after misbehaving they finally get your attention when you spank them. The attention given along with the spanking makes it rewarding. In the case of your child hitting another, one way of not rewarding hitting would be to ignore the negative behavior and give all your attention to the child who was hit.

For children, immediate rewards are the most effective. When you tell your child "Thank you for putting the blocks away" two seconds after it was done, you will be more successful in reinforcing that desirable behavior than if you wait 15 minutes before saying thank you. When you are trying to teach your child appropriate behavior, it is also important not to wait until the child has accomplished the whole task before praising. For example, if you want to teach your child to pick up the blocks after he or she is finished with them, you should start by praising after the first block is put away.

Once you have taught your child a certain behavior, random rewards are the most effective in maintaining it. As your children learn what is expected of them, you can withhold praise until more and more of the task is accomplished. Finally, when they consistently put away all the blocks, you don't need to reinforce their behavior every time. The reward, as a reinforcer, then becomes more effective if it is used randomly, sometimes praising and sometimes not. At this point, not praising is really an expression of confidence that you knew all along they would obey. It's no longer a milestone for them, and only occasional praise and appreciation are necessary or appropriate.

There are two kinds of reinforcers, the social (a smile, a word of praise, a hug) and the nonsocial (points, raisins, stars, etc.). For most children social reinforcement is more important than nonsocial. These are children who have a positive relationship with adults and enjoy pleasing them and having their attention.

For a minority of children it may be necessary to reward them with something more tangible that they desire very highly. For young children something to eat, such as raisins, may be the most effective, or little toys that they can play with immediately. When a child must wait until lunch to eat these reinforcers, or if pennies are given and the child must wait to redeem them, some of the effectiveness of these reinforcers is lost. But in most cases they will still be more meaningful than something abstract such as points or stars. The unique aspect of points or stars is that they can be accumulated. When children have a certain number, they can be traded for something they want very much, such as a toy or a trip to the park. One very effective motivator for children is a chart where they can display their points or stars for accomplishing such tasks as brushing their teeth, cleaning their room, feeding the canary, or saying their memory verse.

When you apply the time-out method, it is important to work on only one behavior at a time. If you try to change too many behaviors at once, the child may resent having to spend so much time in the time-out room or on the time-out chair, and the method becomes a punishment.

In order to evaluate the effectiveness of the discipline, you must know how often the undesirable behavior is happening. This can be done by counting how often it happens in a certain period of time. Then, after the reinforcement program is started, reevaluate your child's behavior periodically to see if any progress has been made.

When you decide to use this type of discipline on a specific behavior with an individual child, it is extremely important that you communicate this to all members of the family so the child can be rewarded or ignored consistently.

Giving your time and attention to children when they are misbehaving tends to reinforce negative behavior. Because of this, there are times when the very best disciplinary action may be to ignore the child, at least during the time of misbehavior. Not every infringement has to be dealt with by immediate action. The following situations might be best handled by ignoring:

1. When children are frustrated or wearing their emotions on their sleeves, the slightest comment may bring an explosion. They will probably be deaf to your pleas anyway. Waiting until they cool down will give them the attention they desire at a time when they are acting appropriately. At this same time, they are also better able to listen and learn.

2. Leave children alone during temper tantrums. Children do not really enjoy throwing them; often they do it only for the effect it has on the parent and the attention it usually brings.

3. When children are deliberately doing something to try to annoy you or get your attention, don't fall into their trap.

4. Ignore behavior you don't like but can tolerate, such as wetting the bed, sucking on a pacifier, or whining. Often children will outgrow these behaviors.

Ignoring your child's misbehavior may be an effective method of modifying it. But ignoring does not mean being indifferent. Although you may deliberately ignore the behavior at the time, you may, a short time later, want to talk to your children about their inappropriate action so there is no misunderstanding about your expectations. If you completely ignore obnoxious behavior, children may view this as passive approval. You must let them know in a positive way that you do not approve of the behavior and will help them learn how to behave in an acceptable way.

Modifying behavior by rewarding the positive and intentionally ignoring the negative does work, but it takes highly involved parents. You must be observant and willing to stop whatever you are doing at the time, to take your child to the time-out area, and to have enough determination to continue the program until your child finally gets the message and demonstrates compliance.

Chapter 13

Shock Therapy

Dear God, grant me the time, patience, and attitude to say, as Jesus did, "Suffer the little children to come unto me," and mean it. Amen.—Kay Kuzma.

Shock therapy is the term I use for a disciplinary method that was espoused in the eighteenth century by French philosopher Jean Rousseau. He said, "Do the opposite of what is usually done and you will almost always be correct." I call this method shock therapy because it is shocking when one does the unexpected. (Note: what I'm talking about has nothing to do with the electrical shock sometimes used on psychotic patients!)

Disciplinary shock therapy can be highly effective in solving problems and preventing conflict, because it gets the child's attention. *But,* unlike other disciplinary methods, it is effective *only* when used very infrequently.

The most common use of shock therapy is in its more negative forms. For example, parents often stop temper tantrums by using negative shocks, such as a spanking, a cold shower, or walking away from the misbehaving child. Why do so many different techniques seem to work? I'm convinced that it is not the technique itself, but the fact that the parents' reaction shocked the child into the realization that the situation was serious. Their behavior was completely unexpected. Indeed, it was the very opposite of what the child expected.

The fact that these techniques are not the parents' customary way of responding is what makes them so effective. But the problem is, the more often they are used, the less effective they become.

For example, although you might effectively give a cold shower to a child once, it would soon cease to be effective if it were used for every inappropriate act. Cold showering (or tossing cold water on the head of a screaming child) and spanking are examples of more negative types of shock therapy, and even though they may prevent conflict in the future, that does not mean that they are the best techniques to use if your final goal is to rear a child with a healthy sense of self-worth. The end (whether a method is effective in producing behavior changes) should never justify the means if a child's feelings of self-worth are damaged in the process.

Positive shock therapy

I highly recommend positive shock techniques. Surprise your children. When they expect you to be angry, smile and willingly forgive. When a spanking is expected, take your child in your lap and cuddle instead. When the child expects to be sent to the time-out room or chair, offer your help in picking up the mess that was made. You'll be pleasantly surprised by the effect of such unexpected parental behavior.

Jeff and his dad were having a tough time communicating. It didn't happen all at once, but gradually during the teen years Jeff's attitude toward his parents became more belligerent. Now, at 15, he didn't confide in them, argued at the drop of a hat, and generally made life miserable with his constant criticism. His folks had imposed consequences by withholding privileges, but it only seemed to make things worse.

One day Jeff's dad noticed a terrific sale on an expensive racing bike—exactly the type Jeff wanted. He was tempted to buy it. Then he argued with himself, "No, Jeff doesn't deserve a bike after the way he has treated me." But the more he thought about it, the more intrigued he became over the effect the gift of a bike might have on Jeff. It was worth the risk. He purchased the bike and took it home.

"Jeff," he called when he got home, "I need your help to unload the van."

"That's all I hear," replied Jeff sarcastically. "'Jeff, do this; Jeff, do that.' You'd think I was a slave or something." Reluctantly Jeff dragged himself out to the van. Dad stood by watching as Jeff started to struggle with the box that contained the bike. Suddenly the writing on the box captured Jeff's attention. "Dad, what's in here? It's not a Guerciotti, is it?"

"Yes," replied Dad. "That's exactly what it is."

"Ahh, well, but Dad, why are you getting a Guerciotti?"

"I bought it for you, son. I knew how much you've been wanting one, and I wanted to make you happy."

"But Dad, I don't deserve it. I've been acting terrible."

"I know, son. You don't deserve it. But I love you in spite of your behavior."

That did it. Jeff's belligerent attitude was broken. He spontaneously hugged his dad and apologized for the terrible way he had been treating him. The bike was an effective surprise.

A mother told me this story: Her 17-year-old son had grown distant. He kept his own schedule, spending more and more time with his peers. His folks tried to impose a curfew, but he just rebelled. One night after they had gone to bed, he came home screaming, "I'm on a bad trip! Don't leave me! Let me sleep with you! Please, don't leave me!" He was frantic.

It was not until then that they realized he had been experimenting with drugs. They called for professional help and were told to watch the boy throughout the night to make sure his breathing and heart rate were stable. They made room for him in their bed and let him sleep between them. All night they rubbed his back, or felt his pulse to make sure he was OK.

In the morning, when the effect of the drugs had worn off, he appeared a changed boy. He couldn't believe what his folks had done for him—even sharing their bed with him—when he deserved harsh punishment.

"I never realized how much you loved me until last night," he said. "When I felt your concerned touch and realized that you were willing to watch over me, in spite of the way I have been behaving, I knew I couldn't continue to hurt you as I've been doing." Once again, it was the shock of positive treatment that turned this teen around.

Caution: Positive shock therapy works, but only if it's used sparingly. For the most part, children need consistent limits, consequences, and other forms of discipline and training to help them learn acceptable behavior. But once in a while a big, positive surprise can work wonders.

What about spanking as a disciplinary method?

Spanking is the most commonly used shock therapy technique. Too many parents spank their children without thinking; they do it just because they feel like it, don't know any better, or believe that a spanking is synonymous with doing the will of the Lord.

Here's an example. The car in front of us was owned by a Christian. We could tell by the bumper stickers "God Loves You" and "Honk if You Love Jesus." On the back window was a rainbow with the words "Praise the Lord."

Inside the car were two young mothers. One was driving and the other was switching. Every few minutes the mom in the passenger seat would turn around to the two preschoolers in the back and switch first one and then the other with a two-foot switch cut from a tree.

If only I could have tuned in on the conversation to detect the reason for such behavior, perhaps I could be more understanding. The children couldn't have been doing too much wrong, strapped in their seats as they were. But whatever it was, that mom was sure giving it to them.

My children couldn't believe what was happening. "What is that woman doing?"

Looking through that rear window with its PTL message, I replied, tongue-in-cheek, "She's praising the Lord and punishing the kids."

My children were indignant. "But that's not how you praise the Lord!"

"Unfortunately," I explained, "there are a lot of parents who read Proverbs 22:15, which says that the rod of correction will drive foolishness far from a child, and figure that if beating a child is good, then the more the better!"

But actually the opposite is true. The more spankings a child receives, the less effective they become. Take my brother, for example. He was always getting a licking, and it didn't change his behavior. In fact, I remember one day he came home and asked Mom to spank him because he broke a neighbor's window. She complied, and a few minutes later he left the house with a clear conscience. He had paid his debt to society. A spanking for him was an easy way out of whatever difficulty he managed to get himself into.

For other children, spankings only increase their defiance. One of the saddest stories I have ever heard was of the little boy who refused to point to his belly button when his parents asked him to. They were encouraged by their friends to spank the child into submission because they erroneously thought, *The Bible says so.* The child either didn't know where his belly button was, or stubbornly refused to play such a foolish game; they ended up beating him to death.

You must realize that some children have become so defiant because of the forceful treatment they have received that they will endure tremendous pain rather than obey. Once you begin physically punishing a child, there is a very thin line between a hard spanking and abuse. And if you spank for the little things, what is there left for really major things such as willful disobedience?

It's especially difficult for me to understand how some people can advocate spanking babies to teach them that they can't have their own way. Spanking babies is abusive.

Most of the time, if babies misbehave it is because they get frustrated, or they just plain don't know any better. Prevention is the best answer. If you can just meet the needs of babies before they get frustrated and out of control, you won't have problems. But even if you do have problems, spanking isn't the answer for infants.

Sally was only 8 months old when she threw her first temper tantrum. Mom could tell Sally was out of control. Why else would she be screaming, kicking, and banging her head? Well, if Sally couldn't control herself, her mom would have to supply the control Sally needed. So she picked Sally up and calmly but firmly held her close until Sally grew tired and relaxed in her arms.

It would have been meaningless to slap Sally, because she was too young to understand why her mother was causing her pain. Spanking a tiny baby for this type of behavior only makes things worse.

Daryl was almost a year old when he discovered the newspaper and started to rip it up. Dad said no in a firm voice, shook his head, and took the newspaper away. When Daryl started to cry, Dad diverted Daryl's attention and then gave Daryl extra attention when he began playing with something appropriate. After a couple weeks Daryl would reach for the paper, hesitate, and shake his head. Daryl was learning that his dad meant what he said. Daryl was learning to choose to be obedient. This type of behavior modification needs to start at a very early age.

But, you ask, why not spank him? Won't he learn a lot faster that way? Why fool around with methods that take more time? Why? Because children will try to avoid pain, and they will not repeat a behavior that brings them enough pain. But spanking doesn't effectively teach children to be self-disciplined.

Occasionally it may be necessary to teach an important, instant lesson of safety by slapping a little hand, for example, that persists in reaching out for the hot burner after you have repeatedly warned the child not to. It's a lot better to do that than to doctor burned hands. However, for most children, just grabbing their hand (instead of slapping it to cause pain) and saying a firm no will teach the same lesson.

Young children catch the wrong message when their parents inflict pain. They associate pain with certain acts and therefore may comply, just as experimental rats will cease painful behavior. But with children, effective discipline includes not only extinguishing inappropriate behavior, but also teaching the child the reason as soon as he or she is old enough to understand.

Some parents spank their babies for age-appropriate behavior, such as wiggling. This is not wise. God made babies to wiggle. Movement is the way they learn. Getting hit for such behavior is confusing. The major lesson babies learn is that the person they are growing to love and trust also causes them pain. They also learn that size and strength are a prerequisite for hitting. Growing up with this type of treatment often makes the children feel bad about themselves and causes mistrust. Are those the lessons you want your baby to learn?

You want your baby to grow up feeling good about himself or herself. Plus, learning to trust Mom and Dad is important, especially during that first year. If there is a chance pain might get in the way of your baby learning these important lessons, why take that chance? Instead, give your babies discipline that isn't likely to have negative side effects.

Other parents spank for misbehavior that could have been avoided if parents had just met the child's need for food or sleep before the child's behavior became uncontrollable. Is it really fair to take your frustrations out on your child when you yourself were the cause?

Spanking is a negative shock technique. It can be effective to get your child's attention concerning the seriousness of the offense, but the more frequently a spanking is used, the less effective it becomes. In fact, I'm convinced that the only parents who use spanking successfully are those who don't spank their children for minor infractions. When a spanking is administered, it surprises the child, gets his or her attention, and motivates the child to choose more appropriate behavior, but in most situations there are better methods to accomplish the same purpose.

There are three major reasons parents spank; none of them have to do with changing the child's behavior: (1) that's the way they were treated and they don't know any better; (2) they're angry; (3) they can't think of anything else to do. A Chinese proverb says it well: "He who strikes the first blow shows he has run out of ideas." If parents would just clearly think through the reasons they spank, most would choose effective disciplinary methods with fewer risk factors.

My friend Elden Chalmers told me about a time he effectively used a "spanking" to change the behavior of an unruly young elementary student. When Elden finally had had enough, he asked the child to stay after school. After the other children had left, Elden said firmly, "This may not happen again. But I don't know what it will take to get you to change. What do you think it will take?"

The child thought for a while and finally said, "You can spank me."

"How many times?" asked Elden.

Again the child thought about it and replied, "Three times."

"How hard?" asked Elden.

The child's lower lip began to quiver and tears formed in his eyes as he said, "Real hard."

"Can you show me how hard is real hard?"

The child swung his hand with force.

"Are you sure three times will do it? Or should it be four or five?"

"No, three will do it!" the child said emphatically, with a tear sliding down his cheek.

"Well," said Elden, "why do I have to spank you at all? If you can make yourself behave after three spanks, why can't you do that now?"

"Oh," the child sighed, "if you don't spank me, I promise I won't do it again."

And that's all it took to turn a stubborn, misbehaving child around. The thought of the spanking was enough to shock him into realizing the seriousness of his misdeeds, and he chose to change.

This example shows that the sorrowful, repentant heart is not dependent upon the actual pain of a spanking, as so many parents believe, but the recognition of the seriousness of the incident. That recognition can be brought about by merely talking about an impending spanking, or by praying with a child before the administration of a spanking. If your goal (to have the child feel sorry for what he or she has done and genuinely repent or cease from the inappropriate actions) can be achieved prior to the spanking, then in love you can "shock" your child and choose not to administer the corporal punishment you had at first intended.

On rare occasions I've spanked my children, but I'm not proud of that fact. I don't think spanking is necessary for effective parenting. I do believe that when a spanking is used, there is probably another more creative method of discipline that would have been just as effective. But if you are at your wit's end, and nothing creative seems to pop into your head, and you feel the urge to spank, please *pray* and then consider carefully these guidelines:

1. *Spank your children only when they are willfully defying your authority and milder measures have failed.* Avoid this method when your children have acted inappropriately because they are too young or im-

mature to know better. Don't automatically spank children for challenging a request you have made. Willful defiance is not the only reason for disobedience. Do not overuse this method.

2. *Never spank your children when you are angry.* It is too easy to spank too hard or too long. There is a very fine line between a hard spanking and child abuse.

3. *Tell your child beforehand whether the spanking is a one-strike, two-strike, or three-strike spanking.* There should never be more than three strikes.

4. *Spank to get your child's attention and impress the child of the seriousness of the offense so you can teach your child a better way.* That's why spankings should come immediately after the misdeed. If you wait too long to administer a spanking, it won't be effective.

5. *Make sure your children clearly understand the reason for the spanking.* Children should be able to feel that their punishment "fits the crime." If they can understand the reason for this disciplinary action, you won't have to contend with feelings of resentment or injustice.

6. *Spank your children in private.* It is demeaning and embarrassing to children to be disciplined in front of an audience.

7. *Your children should experience enough discomfort to change their rebellious attitude.* If after the spanking they slam doors, call you names, or stare you in the eye and say defiantly, "That didn't hurt," the spanking was ineffective. Calmly repeat the spanking once or use a more effective disciplinary technique immediately. Remember, reaction to pain differs in children. Those with fewer pain nerve endings won't feel the pain, so it would be better to teach them by using other methods.

8. *Plan a love experience after the spanking.* If your child is young, take the child in your lap and rock him or her. If older, go to the child in five or 10 minutes. If the child is not yet ready to talk, return in another five minutes. Talk about pleasant things. Offering your time and tenderness after such an experience will convince your child of your love. But beware. If the only time children receive love is after a spanking, they can come to the erroneous conclusion that to get love they have to endure pain, which sets them up to be victims of abusive relationships.

9. *Consider your child's age.* In order for this technique to be effective, your child must be old enough to realize that this isn't your usual method of disciplining. He or she must be able to reason from cause to effect to see the justice of this type of discipline. An older child's self-worth can be shattered by a spanking. It can be a demeaning experience. I would caution you to avoid spanking before your children are 2 and after they are 8 or 9.

10. Finally, *the rapport you have with your children will determine whether or not you can safely use spanking as a method of shock therapy.* Diana Baumrind, a psychologist, has found that spanking produces passivity, timidity, and fearful conformity when it is used impulsively by repressive, restrictive parents. But when parents are warm, responsive,

flexible, and have a good rapport with their children, an occasional spanking as fair discipline is linked to self-reliant, independent, and confident behavior (reported in *Today's Child,* November 1978).

The following statement by the nineteenth-century inspirational writer Ellen White has had a big influence on my thinking: "Whipping may be necessary when other resorts fail, yet she [the mother] should not use the rod if it is possible to avoid doing so. But if milder measures prove insufficient, punishment that will bring the child to its senses should in love be administered. Frequently *one such correction will be enough for a lifetime,* to show the child that he does not hold the lines of control" *(Child Guidance,* p. 250; italics supplied).

Should you spank or shouldn't you?

Some say spanking is biblical. There are a number of texts that speak of the "rod of correction." But it is clear the admonition to use the "rod" was the admonition to use corrective measures, not merely a sanction to beat a child. For example, the last half of Proverbs 23:13 says, "For if you beat him with a rod, he will not die." We all know that that phrase, if taken out of context, is not true. Thousands of children each year are dying from beatings they have received from the hands of their parents. The text must be understood in relationship to the first half: "Do not withhold correction from a child." Disciplinary correction is the principle we must follow, not the literal beating of our children. We must correct and discipline our children, just as God does us ("For whom the Lord loves He corrects," Prov. 3:12). Rather than taking isolated texts and trying to prove or disprove spanking, it is much more productive to look at the principles underlying texts such as:

"He who spares the rod hates his son, but he who loves him disciplines him promptly" (Prov. 13:24).

"Foolishness is bound up in the heart of a child; the rod of correction will drive it far from him" (Prov. 22:15).

"The rod and rebuke give wisdom, but a child left to himself brings shame to his mother" (Prov. 29:15).

Some suggest that the biblical "rod of correction" was a standard measuring instrument to determine certain standards. The analogy could be made that if children didn't meet the standards, the "rod" would be used to make the necessary corrections—not by beating, but by pointing out error!

Basically, the biblical principle is that if you fail to correct your children, you dishonor God, do a disservice to society, and destroy your child's chance for a meaningful, productive, self-disciplined life.

Proverbs 29:17 sums it up nicely: "Correct your son, and he will give you rest; yes, he will give delight to your soul."

Perhaps it will help you to make a better decision about spanking if you focus on Jesus. Only once do we see Him with a switch in His hand, and that was to drive the corrupt money changers out of His Father's Temple.

How would Jesus have handled those children in the back seat of the

PTL car? Can you in your wildest imagination see Him hitting them?

Focusing on Jesus as a disciplinarian, I see the Good Shepherd with His sheep. I see Him going out of His way to find and carry home the lost ones. I see Him meeting every physical need. (The Shepherd of the twenty-third psalm found green grass and still water for His sheep.) Sheep are known to be pretty stubborn, but I see Him using His staff, not to beat on the behinds of the little lambs, but to protect them from predators and nudge them in the way they should go. How else could David, the one-time lost sheep, end up saying, "Thy rod and thy staff they comfort me"?

I see Jesus calling to a disobedient child, "Come unto Me." Then I see Him gently lifting that child into His arms and taking time to talk with him. I hear Jesus pointing out the folly of disobedience and the consequences that will result. Then I see Jesus pointing out the love that God has for His erring children and how God established limits so boys and girls wouldn't hurt one another. Then I see Jesus, with tears in His eyes, praying with that little one that he will turn from disobedience and be willing to obey his folks' rules, and God's. And then as the little one runs off to play, I see Jesus noticing the good things he does and giving that child a smile of approval.

The reason I wrote *Easy Obedience* was to present a more gentle, Christlike approach to rearing children. Should you spank your children? You'll have to decide what's best for your own children. But if you make an occasional mistake, don't be overwhelmed with guilt. Children are resilient when they know they are loved, and they are quick to forgive when they know you're trying to do your very best to be the kind of parent God wants you to be. Reassure yourself with this jingle:

"The definition of perfect parenting is easy to express—just err and err and err again, but less and less and less."

Chapter 14

Problem Solving Through Negotiation

We are adding a greater burden to society than we could ever compensate for with all our good deeds if we don't spend time training our children, time helping them to be secure as people.—Pat King, How Do You Find the Time?

"Children, obey your parents." That may be a biblical admonition (Eph. 6:1), but the older your children, the more they would like to be included in the decisions that affect them.

I vowed to honor and obey when I said "I do" and married Jan, but I would still be resentful if I felt Jan were pushing me by demanding, "Pick up the laundry, mail this package, and invite these people over for Saturday night." I'd much rather hear him say, "Honey, I'm very busy today, but I think I can be home for dinner on time if you could pick up the laundry, mail this package, and invite the guests for Saturday night. Would that be possible?" I'd much rather be asked than told.

Children feel the same way. If you involve them in decisions that concern them, they will be much more willing to comply with your requests. That's why moms and dads need to become experts in the art of negotiation.

It takes time to discuss and negotiate solutions. That's why so many parents simply tell their children, "Do it or else!" But negotiating is well worth the time it takes, because it overcomes negative resistance, since it involves both parties in determining the solution to a problem. It allows for compromise and creative solutions. Plus, negotiation often results in a contract so that both parties know exactly what is expected of the other. That limits the hurt feelings when the consequence clause must be imposed.

Six steps for problem solving

In order for negotiation to be effective, a child must be (1) verbal enough to discuss possible solutions; (2) smart enough to understand what is being contracted for; and (3) mature enough to keep the bargain that is made. How does negotiation work? Follow these steps:

Step 1: *Define the problem with your child.* For example, John has not been brushing his teeth regularly, and he rebels at every reminder. So you approach him about his behavior. "John, I have to pay the dentist's bills, and when you don't brush your teeth the bills can increase. What can we do together to make sure that this important job gets done?"

Step 2: *Brainstorm together about possible solutions to the problem.* Do not evaluate each suggestion as it is made, or it will diminish the creativity. Wait until all possible solutions are on the table. Working together, you might come up with the following list: put a reminder note on the bathroom mirror; do not serve dessert anymore until John begins to brush regularly; buy an electric toothbrush; get better-tasting toothpaste; have a special code as a reminder; give John a nickel every time he brushes and have him return a nickel if he forgets.

Step 3: *Decide together which possibility is most acceptable.* It's at this step that you begin to evaluate the brainstorming suggestions. Now you or your child can say that certain ideas are not acceptable and one by one cross them off the list. Whenever possible be open to compromise. Sometimes combining aspects of different solutions may be meaningful. The more dogmatic you are, the more stubborn you will find your children will be, and the less chance there will be for a successful resolution to be reached.

Here's a possible solution to the problem of John's not brushing his teeth. John thinks that he would remember if he had an electric toothbrush. If he forgets, John promises that he won't get angry if he is reminded with the code words "Billy Goat." When he hears the code, he will brush his teeth immediately. A consequence clause should be included at this point, such as if he resists after being reminded, he must forgo dessert at the next meal.

Step 4: *Decide when the contract will be put into effect and when evaluated.* Many times agreements are made and forgotten. It helps to make it clear when the agreement starts and when it will be evaluated. John's mom might say, "Let's start this agreement tomorrow morning. Is that OK? And one week from today let's talk about how things are going. I'll mark it on our family calendar."

Step 5: *Indicate in some manner that you both agree on the contract.* Write it down, sign it, shake hands, or seal it with a kiss. This symbolic gesture of agreement is like a seal to the agreement and promotes compliance.

Step 6: *Evaluate the effectiveness of the contract periodically.* For many agreements you might want to monitor compliance daily for the first week or so, and then on a less frequent schedule as the behavior becomes habitual. If the contract is not working, go back to the bargaining table and draw up a new contract.

Negotiating a contract involves a child in the decision-making process. It is excellent training for a child's inner control system—a necessity for self-discipline. The following guidelines will help you use this method most effectively:

1. *Don't approach a problem by placing blame solely on your child.* This only antagonizes children and prevents a successful resolution. Instead of blaming, put the emphasis on how something affects you. Start your message with the pronoun "I." For example, "I get upset and angry when I hear so much quarreling." This is much less offensive to a child than an accusing "you" message such as "You kids quit quarreling right now. All you do is fight with each other."

2. *Be willing to bargain.* Every problem has a solution. If it doesn't, it's not a problem; it's reality. Come to the bargaining table with a positive attitude that a solution can be found. Be flexible. Parents who are rigid and are willing to settle for only the one solution they think is best will sabotage this problem-solving process.

3. *Be supportive, not antagonistic.* Show your child by your behavior and attitude that you are the ally, not the enemy.

Negotiation can be used for determining appropriate consequences. Decide ahead of time, through negotiation, what should be the consequence for a certain misbehavior. For example, no supper until the dog has been fed, no TV until the homework is done, or if you don't help with the meal preparation, you must do the dishes. Once children agree on these consequences, then when they goof up all you have to ask is "What did we decide should be the consequence for this?" Children can't (or shouldn't) argue with the fairness of this type of discipline once they have agreed to it.

Caution: You must be sure your children agree to the contract because they feel that the consequence is fair—not just because they fear your anger and rejection. You never win if your children give resentful compliance. This leads only to hostility and later rebellion. As a parent you don't want mere compliance from your children—you want *willing* compliance. Otherwise, you'll find yourself pushing your children to obey and will end up getting resistance.

Negotiating contracts

The White family is a good example of how negotiating contracts can creatively solve your discipline problems. The Whites' family policy had always been that the children should earn the money they needed for school activities and other items above and beyond the basic necessities. They did this by taking on jobs around the house. Mom kept a list of jobs, with the amount of money she was willing to give for each one.

The system worked well until Linda's sophomore year in high school, when she decided she was too grown-up to help around the house. She had more important things to do than earn extra money for spending. But at the same time her "want" list doubled, and she soon depleted her savings. That's when Linda began taking advantage of her parents. Band tour was coming up. She needed $75. Then there was a varsity jacket, a new dress, and shoes for the banquet. When Mom restated the family policy that she should be earning this extra money, Linda willingly agreed. But she needed the money now. What was she supposed to do?

Mom bailed her out the first couple times and lent her the money. But Linda, even though she had plenty of opportunity to do odd jobs around the house to earn the money to pay her mom back, took no responsibility for her debt. Mom decided that she'd give no more loans. But Linda desperately needed the money. They had come to an impasse. It was time to head to the negotiation table to see how the problem could be solved. The result was the following loan agreement, which would encourage the children to earn their necessary spending money before they needed it.

Loan Agreement

- I agree that whenever I borrow money I will pay a 10 percent loan origination fee.
- I understand that I will be allowed two days for every $5 lent to pay the loan back in full, and that for every day late a 10 percent late fee will be charged.
- I also understand that no further credit will be extended until each loan is repaid.

Signed: ______________________________

____

Date: ________________________

The family also decided that it would be important to work out a plan so that the children could begin early to earn the money they knew they would be needing for future activities. For example, Linda's brother wanted to attend three weeks of summer camp, which would cost $100 each week for a total of $300. See the contract they worked up for him on the next page.

At the same negotiation session, Mom came up with another contract that would allow the children another way to earn money. She really wanted to encourage her children to read their Bibles. This was so important to her that she said she would be willing to give them $1 for every chapter read. Then she made up tally sheets for them to record the chapter read and the date completed. The children loved the new challenge and eagerly dusted off their Bibles!

Contract to Earn Money for Summer Camp

- I will earn the sum of $100 per camp week, for a total of $300.
- I will earn the total amount per camp before I attend. If I do not earn the necessary amount, I will forfeit the camp.
- If I have earned the total of $300 two weeks before summer camp is to begin, then I understand Mom and Dad will give me $25 for spending money.

Signed: ______________________________

____

Date: ________________________

Using incentives

If our values and principles are not violated, most of us can be "bought" for a price. If someone makes a deal sweet enough, we go for it. It's not that we've been forced against our wills; we choose. We change our priorities because the rewards are worth it.

There may be times that it is very important to you that your child does a certain thing that he or she really doesn't want to do. There is the potential of a major battle, because your child doesn't hold the same values or priorities as you do, or doesn't see the relative importance of what you've asked. You know you could force the issue, but that would likely result in hard feelings and resentment. It would be more pleasant for all if the child would willingly do it, not because he or she wants to, but because there are enough rewards to make compliance worthwhile.

I don't believe in bribes. A bribe is something offered that causes people to do something against their will. Parents who bribe their children to obey have basically lost control. Why should children obey willingly if they know that if they hold out, throw a temper tantrum, or resist in some way their parents will give them a reward? Bribes, although getting the immediate behavior you desire, basically reinforce negative behavior. And like blackmail, the more often you bribe, the costlier it becomes as the receiver demands more and more for compliance.

However, there is nothing wrong with an incentive. An incentive is something that motivates children to be willing to do what you ask. It sweetens the deal, so to speak. An incentive is often a part of a negotiated contract. Parents should be quick to offer their children incentives for appropriate behavior. "If you finish picking up your toys by 3:00, we'll stop by the park for you to feed the ducks." An incentive is basically a positive parent-imposed consequence for obedience. An incentive is most effective if it is given randomly throughout the day, rather than for every request a parent makes. You don't want your children to hold out until you have to add to the incentive. An occasional reward adds a positive element to the parent-child relationship and helps children maintain a compliant attitude.

The difference between a bribe and an incentive is not necessarily the value of what is offered, but the attitude of the receiver. An incentive is given for willing obedience. A bribe is given for obedience, regardless of a child's attitude.

Here's one time that I successfully used an incentive with my teenage son:

Kimberly, our oldest, was getting married, and I was looking forward to the family pictures that would be taken. However, I was embarrassed by Kevin's long, unruly hair. When I had previously mentioned that Kevin cut his hair, he had basically cried, "Never!" so I knew there was the possibility of a confrontation. Here's how I approached it:

"Kevin, I am spending a lot of money for the family pictures that will be taken at Kim's wedding, and I want everyone looking their best. I know you like your hair long and don't want it cut. But I like it short. I don't want to fight with you and force you to cut it, but what would it take for you to get your hair cut willingly to please your mom?"

Kevin said he wanted a new surfboard. I agreed to pay half. A deal was struck, and Kevin willingly went to the barber. I'll admit it was an expensive haircut, but it was worth every cent. Every time I look at those pictures, I'm so thankful he cut his hair. There was no forcing, no anger, no resentment, no conflict. And, as I admitted to Kevin after the haircut, I would probably have helped him finance his new surfboard anyway. He laughed.

An incentive is a way to give the child a choice. "You must do your homework; you have no choice about that. But you do have a choice about whether you want me to punish you with a consequence if you don't get it done, or if you want me to give you something special as a reward for doing it." When you give children the choice between the consequence of punishment versus the reward of an incentive, they will choose the latter. Negotiate with your children. Go through the pros and cons of certain choices. Strike a deal, even sweetening it if that's necessary, and enjoy a win-win relationship with your children.

Using freedom to make choices as a negotiating tool

As your children reach their teen years and ask for permission to do various things, or want to make their own decisions, consider the responsible behavior you want from them, and ask for it in exchange.

"Mom, may I go surfing Friday afternoon?" Kevin asks on Tuesday.

"Sure, Kevin, if all your Friday chores are done before you leave." Guess what? Those chores are done on Wednesday.

◆◆◆

"Dad, can I use the car tonight?" Carl asks.

"I was going to wash the car, but if you don't mind doing it, I'll let you use the car for two hours."

◆◆◆

"Can I invite Larry to go with us this weekend?"

"Sure, but you'll need to willingly include your sister in your activities so she won't feel left out."

◆◆◆

"I want to make my own decisions about how I use my money."

"You can do that as long as you save one third and are willing to show me your savings account on a regular basis."

You'll find many more ideas about how to exchange freedom for responsibility in chapter 15.

Family council meeting

There is a reason businesses have staff meetings, football teams have their huddles, organizations hold conferences, and doctors have rounds. The reason? To communicate, to build rapport, to share information, to formulate plans, to make decisions, to solve problems. Families should have a regular weekly meeting time for these very same reasons. Here's a typical agenda for a family council meeting:

Family Council Agenda

Devotional thought (story) and prayer
Words of appreciation and thanks for different family members
Review of week's activities
Plans
Discussion items (submitted during the week)
Problems that need to be solved (steps to problem solving)
Favorite dessert
Family activity, game, or puzzle

You can see by reading down the agenda items that a successful family council meeting has a broad agenda that includes a devotional time, favorite food, the business of plans for the future and problems that must be solved, as well as some fun and games. It should be an enjoyable time, one that the family looks forward to.

To make it successful, each family member must make a commitment to attend. For some families an early-morning breakfast time may be the only time to get the entire family together. Others may choose the weekend. But the important thing is that you not let anything interfere.

Problem solving takes time. It takes time to negotiate and develop contracts. Many times families neglect this important aspect of training their children for self-discipline because there just isn't enough time. It's easier to simply tell the kids what to do and impose consequences for disobedience than to discuss problem issues, plan future behavior, and involve the children in determining appropriate consequences for breaking agreements. But consider the long-term benefits when families have a weekly meeting:

1. Children feel they are an important part of the family government and decision-making process.
2. Problems are never more than a week away from a solution.
3. Children gain experience in carrying leadership responsibilities, communicating ideas, practicing listening skills, and being a part of negotiations and problem solving.
4. Parents and children gain a better understanding of each other.
5. The family that prays and plays together stays together!

The older your children are, the more you will enjoy negotiating contracts as a way of solving problems. Master the technique early so you'll be able to get as much use out of it as possible. Start today by writing down an offensive or irresponsible behavior that your child might be willing to change with an attractive contract. Don't delay. Head to the bargaining table.

Chapter 15

Freedom for Responsibility

If you want your children to keep their feet on the ground, put some responsibility on their shoulders.—Abigail Van Buren.

Kevin was 12 and we were still telling him when to go to bed, because if he didn't get his sleep he was miserable the next day. One night Kevin rebelled. "I hate it when you tell me to go to bed. You don't tell the girls."

"That's because they go to bed at a reasonable time," I answered.

"It's not fair . . ."

I knew we were headed down the road to an endless argument if I didn't change my approach. So I said, "Kevin, I really don't care when you go to bed as long as you wake up with your own alarm, get dressed without me reminding you, help make the lunches, eat breakfast with the family, and have a pleasant attitude. In fact, you can go to bed any time you want as long as you can come home from school with energy enough to do your homework and help your mom."

"Really?" His eyes were wide with the anticipation of freedom—freedom to choose his own bedtime.

"Yes, Kevin. In fact, if you want to start tonight it's fine with me. And if you can act the way I mentioned for seven days in a row, I'll never again tell you when you should go to bed."

That first night I went to bed about 11:00 and had to bite my tongue to not say something to Kevin. I have no idea when he finally turned off the light, but I was sure I'd have to pull him out of bed the next morning and the deal would be off.

But he was up at the crack of dawn, dressed, helped fix his sisters' lunches, and was the first one to the breakfast table. I was shocked. I knew, however, he'd blow it when he came home from school. He would be miserable because he hadn't gotten enough sleep. But the minute he got home from school his first words were, "Mom, what can I do for you today?" I nearly fainted. I gave him a few tasks. He then went in, did his homework, and promptly fell asleep at 6:00 p.m. But he made it through the first day . . . and the second. And seven days later he had earned the freedom to determine his own bedtime.

I have discovered that children will do almost anything to get their freedom. Most end up fighting for it and eventually win it, as their parents' endurance wears down and the teenagers become more and more uncontrollable. But there is a better way. Wave the banner over your front door, post it on the walls, shout it from the rooftop: *Freedom for Responsibility.* Be generous in dishing out freedom to your children; just be sure they earn it by acting in a responsible way.

Giving freedom for responsibility will keep you from feeling like a nagging ninny standing over your children, telling them every move to make. "Brush your teeth, make your bed, empty the trash." You probably hate being bossy as much as or more than your children hate your being bossy. Nagging will never turn irresponsible children into responsible ones, but I know four powerful strategies that will.

Responsibility strategy number one: being your own boss

The first strategy for teaching responsibility has to do with encouraging your children to be their own boss.

Bossing can become an irritating way of life, a trap that older, more capable family members fall into. I know. It's happened to us. When Kevin was younger, he had a mom and dad and two big sisters, all telling him what to do. But it wasn't until 6-year-old cousin Jennifer asked "Why does everyone boss Kevin around?" that we recognized how bossy we had become. I decided I'd have to do something to encourage Kevin to take responsibility for his own behavior. So one night as I was tucking him into bed I asked, "Kevin, do you like getting bossed around?"

"No," he said emphatically.

"Then you've got to be your own boss. Nobody will boss you around if you take control of your own life. When you do what you're supposed to do, nobody has to nag you. So whose fault is it that you get bossed?"

"Mine, I guess," he said sheepishly.

"That's right. Either you be your own boss and tell yourself what to do, or somebody else will have to boss you."

"But it's hard," sighed Kevin. "I don't like to do all the things I have to do."

"The things still have to be done. So either you take control of your life or we'll boss you around. What will it take to get your boss to work?"

"Well, Mom, remember that little truck with the motorcycles in the back?"

"OK, that will be your boss's salary for two full days of work. I'll help you make a list each morning. You have until noon to prove that your boss is working. No one will remind or nag. But at noon, if your boss is not doing his job, then the rest of the family has the right to begin bossing you around, and that day won't count toward your truck. Remember, it has to be two full days in a row! Do you think your boss is strong enough to handle you?"

"I think so."

I leaned over and kissed his forehead. "Your boss will need a lot of rest. He'll be taking over the job of four people. Instead of everybody else bossing you around, he'll have to do it all by himself. Good night, boss," I whispered as I closed the door.

Well, two days later Kevin's boss had earned his salary, the truck with the motorcycles in the back. The biggest problem was retraining Kevin's four previous bosses! But with Kevin taking responsibility for his own life, we soon settled back into our proper roles of controlling ours.

Getting your children to take responsibility for their own behavior by becoming their own bosses is an especially helpful technique for young children. But I've discovered an even more effective strategy for when children get older.

Responsibility strategy number two: retraining your parent strategy

There are many children who resent how their parents treat them, and they blame their parents. What they don't realize is that their parents are probably treating them exactly the way irresponsible children deserve to be treated. But if you say that straight out, children won't buy it. So I enjoy challenging kids with the fact that they have the power to change their parents. It may be hard to "teach an old dog new tricks," but it is possible. And it's the same with parents. They're not easy to retrain. But sometimes it's important to try. Here's how strategy number two works.

I once met a teenager who complained bitterly about the way his father treated him. "Dad never says he loves me or asks how my day went; he just constantly tells me things to do. Whenever he sees me, he says something like 'Jack, help your mother set the table,' or 'Jack, have you fed the dog yet?' I'm so sick of it that I try to hide when he comes home and avoid him as much as I can."

"Wow," I replied. "You've got a real problem, don't you?"

"I sure do," he mumbled. "Why does he have to pick on me? He never says those things to my brothers. They can be sitting in the same room, but I'm always the one who gets told what to do."

As I listened I began to put the pieces together. Jack's brothers were always busy. They had certain responsibilities that they carried out without being asked, and when they weren't busy with their chores, they were either practicing their musical instruments, doing their homework, or shooting baskets to make varsity.

Jack, on the other hand, shirked responsibility. He hated to do chores, so he always waited until his dad got on his case before he did what he needed to do. Jack admitted that he didn't like to practice, so he put it off as long as possible. Play came first, and homework was tackled only when he was threatened or forced. So by shirking responsibilities,

Jack had trained his dad to tell him what to do, and a negative pattern of interaction had developed.

"Well," I said to Jack, "it seems to me you've got a big job ahead. You've trained your dad to treat you like this, and now you've got to retrain him to treat you the way you want to be treated."

"Yeah, I sure wish I could. But Dad will never change."

"Hey, don't say that. He's not like that to your brothers, so it seems to me it's your problem. And it's your responsibility to retrain him."

"How do I do that?"

"Simple," I said. "You figure out what your dad wants you to do, and do it before he has a chance to tell you. If you know he wants you to feed the dog before he gets home from work, then do it. When he gets home and says 'Jack, feed the dog,' all you have to say is 'I already did it.' After a week or two of your saying 'I already did it,' chances are he won't feel he needs to remind you anymore, so he won't."

"But what if I don't want to feed the dog?"

"Well, if it's your responsibility, and you don't want to do it, then I guess you'll just have to put up with your dad's bugging you. It's all up to you. Tell you what, Jack. Why don't you try it for a week? Do everything you should do before your dad has a chance to tell you, and see if it doesn't make a difference in the way he treats you. I think your dad's a pretty smart guy. I have a feeling he can be retrained."

Well, Jack took me up on my challenge and is enjoying a new relationship with his dad. It was worth the extra effort it took to retrain his dad.

If you have a child suffering from this same problem, having to live with a parent who needs "retraining," why don't you share this strategy, and challenge your child to see if he or she can't retrain you? Parents can learn new tricks!

Responsibility strategy number three: acting adult

Transactional analysis (TA) is a psychological theory that focuses on why people behave the way they do in various interactions. TA can help you and your children analyze why they react the way they do when pushed instead of led, and it can help your children to act more responsibly.

This is the theory behind TA: Each person has three styles of personality within himself or herself.

1. The *parent* personality is one of superiority. It occurs when a person feels he or she knows best and lets other people know. It's opinionated, bossy, degrading, and unwilling to listen to other viewpoints. It makes others feel inferior. You speak from your parent personality when you say "That's no way to do it," "Watch out," "You never were very good at that," "You should think before doing."

2. The *child* personality is one of inferiority. It's an immature personality: emotional, impulsive, and irresponsible. This personality is exhibited when one jumps to conclusions, acts on emotions, rebels,

belittles oneself, or fails to make decisions. The child personality might say such things as "I hate it when you do that," "Don't tell me what to do," "It wasn't my fault," "I always make mistakes," "I don't know how to do it," "You're always right." The child personality is the way youngsters (or grown-ups) usually act when they feel pushed.

3. The *adult* personality is the mature, thinking personality that treats others as equals. When you operate in this personality it makes people feel good about themselves, and the result is that they usually treat you in the same respectful way. If you could just learn to always interact with your children using your adult personality, you would probably experience very little conflict. But the problem is that your parent or your child too often dominates your interaction.

The parent personality in you almost always causes the child personality to respond, no matter what the age of the person. For example: "Put those shoes away right now" (your parent) usually causes the child to respond in his or her child personality: "Don't tell me what to do" or "I don't know how."

In contrast, your child personality almost always causes the parent personality of the other to respond. For example: "I've had it with you kids!" (your child) might get a response such as "Mom, that's no way to behave" or "What happened is your fault," which would be your child's parent personality speaking.

Once you explain TA to your children, they can have a better understanding of why they may be getting treated the way they are and can begin accepting some of the responsibility for the conflicts they have been having with Mom or Dad.

Travis, a very wise father, used TA to try to prevent further conflicts that his son, Justin, was having with his mom. Mom was on the warpath. Justin had promised to have his room picked up by breakfast time and to feed the animals and finish his homework before 8:00 each evening without any reminders. In return, Mom had promised to let Justin decide on his own bedtime.

But Justin thought that at 14 years of age he should be able to set his own bedtime, regardless of what he did during the day. Each night the battle over bedtime grew more intense. Finally Mom declared to Dad that she had had it, and she was giving Justin a checklist of duties that he had to do or there were going to be severe penalties. Dad knew that Justin and his mother had been on such lousy terms that the checklist at this time would infuriate Justin. So, trying to divert a catastrophic battle, Travis went into his son's bedroom just after he had gone to bed, sat down next to him, and began to talk. Travis reviewed TA with Justin.

"Now, if a person is behaving in his child personality by being irresponsible and spouting off impulsive statements, how is the other person likely to respond?"

"In their parent," Justin responded correctly.

"And how does the parent act?"

"Bossy and superior—like they know it all," said Justin.

"And how is a person likely to respond to this bossy parent?"

"In his child personality, by saying whatever pops into his head and being childish."

"And if you don't want someone to respond in his parent, what do you need to do to get him to act in his adult?"

"React in your adult." Justin knew TA theory well.

"OK, Justin, let me explain what's about to happen tomorrow morning. You have been acting like a child all week, not carrying your part of the bargain to clean your room, feed the pets, and get your homework done. So your mother has been acting as a parent, treating you like a child, forcing you to go to bed at the time she has decided. And the result? You've been acting like a child and rebelling.

"Your mother now is so angry that she has decided to give you a checklist, with a severe penalty attached, which is a typical parent response.

"But chances are you're not going to like that. You now have the choice of acting like a child and making your mother act even more like a parent, or you can surprise her and act like an adult and bring her back to her adult, so she will be kind and understanding to you. It's up to you."

"What do you think I ought to do to get her into her adult?" asked Justin.

"Well, if I were you, I'd get up first thing in the morning, clean my room, and offer to help her with breakfast. That would be acting in your adult, in a very responsible way. Then I'd bring up the subject and say something like 'Mom, I've been thinking that I've been very irresponsible this past week, and I'd like to apologize.' And I have a feeling if you continue to act in your adult that your mom may even forget about making you a checklist. But if she doesn't and you still get a checklist, say, 'Thanks, Mom, this will make it a lot easier for me to remember what I should be doing.' And if you continue to act in your adult, I don't think you'll have any more trouble."

The next morning a very responsible Justin approached his mom in a very adult way, and the crisis was averted.

Once children get the idea that they have this kind of power over their parents—that they can change bossy parents into civil ones—then acting responsibly isn't work, it's a game of behaving so you can keep Mom and Dad acting like adults!

It's really fun when you begin using your understanding of TA to monitor your own actions and words so you don't evoke the child or the parent in others. Remember, you've got to act in your adult if you want your children to respond in their adult!

Once the whole family gets into TA, you can begin analyzing why family members are acting the way they are and without criticizing say, "Oops, your parent is showing!" or "Careful, I think I may have heard your child responding." It becomes a game. Your children will love "correcting" you. When you become aware of how your behavior affects others, you'll be more careful to stay in your adult, so your children will be more apt to respond in their adult! Remember, your adult personality doesn't get angry and threaten or push and punish. Adult personalities are masters at leading others in the way they should go, and the result is a lot more compliance. Why don't you play a little TA with your family today?

Responsibility strategy number four: SEA decision-making method

Children become good decision-makers by making decisions. But just how early can you give them this responsibility? When can you trust your child to make good decisions? Try the SEA decision-making strategy and find out.

At a very early age children can learn to make simple decisions. They should be making their own decisions if they can *seek* the information they need to make a good decision, *evaluate* the alternatives without bias, and *accept* the consequences of their decisions. The acronym to remember is SEA—S for seeking information, E for evaluating the alternatives, and A for accepting the consequences.

Here is how this strategy works. Let's say your 3-year-old wants to run out into a busy street. You don't allow her to make such a decision. She is too young to understand or seek the crucial information about the speed and momentum of moving vehicles relative to 3-year-old legs. Evaluating the pros and cons of running into the street is beyond her ability, and the consequences are too severe. So you impose your own decision.

But the same 3-year-old may be ready to make a simple, nonthreatening choice, such as whether or not to eat between meals. My daughter Kim made this choice when she was 3. She wanted a cookie. I said no. She insisted. She nagged. So I put the SEA decision-making strategy to a test.

I gave her information on why I disapproved of her eating cookies between meals. When her tummy was filled with a sugary cookie, it wouldn't be hungry for the healthy food that we'd be having for supper. The alternatives I gave her were simple: have one cookie now and nothing for supper, or two cookies as dessert after supper. The consequences of eating a cookie before supper were not life-threatening. Yes, she might not be hungry for supper, and it could even lead to a habit (which she'd have to overcome later) of snitching junk food between meals, but none of the consequences were great enough for me to feel that she wasn't capable of making the decision. So after I was sure she understood the consequences, I allowed her to decide.

No more nagging. She decided it would be better to wait until supper.

I can't promise that your child will make a similar decision. At the time I was unsure about Kim. I had no way of knowing what she would do. And I'm smart enough to know that even though it works once, it might not continue to work. But a child needs to be given the opportunity to learn how to struggle with decision-making. Indispensable to learning is the need to make poor decisions and suffer the consequences!

Some children pick up the SEA decision-making strategy quickly and become mature decision-makers at a surprisingly early age. You may have a precocious child. But you will never know until you take the risk yourself and put SEA to the test.

One of the biggest areas of conflict between parents and older children is over decision-making. Children need to become independent and learn to make good decisions on their own, but when it comes to major decisions, too many parents take over.

Just how far would you go in allowing your children to make decisions on their own? Would you allow them to decide such things as whether or not they needed a curfew time? With the SEA strategy you should be fairly safe. But you have to make sure your children can get all the information they need, will not be biased as they consider the alternatives, and will not suffer consequences that are too severe. Sometimes it might take a little creativity to make sure that they can get all the information—including the possible consequences. Here's what happened to one family who decided to trust their children's decision-making abilities:

During the children's early years Mom and Dad made most of the major decisions for the family, but now that the children were in their teens the parents felt that they should have a say. So it was decided that a curfew policy would be discussed at the family council meeting and then voted on. The majority would win. Now this took a lot of parental faith in the decision-making ability of their three children, because the parents could get outvoted.

The parents knew that if they gave their children enough information and the reasons a curfew was important, they'd vote for a reasonable curfew. The matter was discussed at length at the council meeting, and Dad called for the vote: three to two, the children outvoted their parents. No curfew.

Mom was beside herself. Enough of this democratic stuff. "I can't live not knowing where the kids are or what time they will return."

"Just a minute," said Dad. "The children just don't have enough information yet." And then Mom and Dad sat down and planned a way for their teenagers to get the information they needed to make a good decision.

The next afternoon, without telling the children, Mom packed her suitcase and left the house, planning to spend the night with friends. About suppertime the teens began to ask, "Where's Mom? We're starved."

"Well," said Dad, "since your mom isn't home, you kids better get something to eat."

Throughout the evening hours, they kept wondering where Mom could be, but they really became worried about 10:30 p.m.

"Dad, where could Mom be? Even K Mart's closed!"

"She's a big girl," replied Dad. "I think she can take care of herself. Go on to bed and don't worry."

Early the next morning the children rushed into their parents' bedroom and found only Dad. "Mom still isn't here? Where could she be?"

"I was just wondering that myself," said Dad.

Just as three frantic teenagers were rushing to the phone to report a missing mom, in she walked, suitcase in hand.

"Mom, where have you been?" they shouted. "And why didn't you come home last night?"

"I thought," she replied, "we voted we didn't have to tell anyone where we were going or what time we would return."

"But Mom, you're a *mother!*" And then light began to dawn. Immediately they called a family council and voted five to zero for a curfew. They wanted to know where their mother was going and what time she'd return.

It's true: children *can* make good decisions on their own, if they have enough information. I take my hat off to these creative parents, who, instead of forcing an issue and then perhaps having to deal with three defiant teenagers, figured out a way to help their children gain the information they needed to make a responsible decision.

The way you raise responsible children is to get out of the driver's seat, so to speak, and let them take over the wheel. If you continue to stay in charge by constantly nagging, reminding, and making decisions for your children, they'll let you take over their responsibility, hoping someday you'll forget to remind them, and then if something doesn't get done it's your fault for not reminding them.

Put the responsibility on their shoulders by using one of the above strategies. Then clearly spell out the consequences of what will happen if they fail to carry out their responsibilities. As children get older, they can even help to determine what would be appropriate consequences. And if they fail, let them suffer the consequences. It may sound cruel, but it can be a powerful lesson!

Let your child know that there are many ways that people help themselves to remember what they need to do. One is to make a list. Another is to group tasks around a certain part of the day, such as "things to do before breakfast." Certain tasks can become habitual when you get in a good routine. If nothing else works, encourage your child to simply ask someone, "Is there anything else I need to do now?" If your child can't remember, there's a good chance someone else can.

Sometimes children unconsciously neglect certain tasks because they hate them. Check with your children. If that's their problem, you can almost always come up with a compromise. Trade one of your tasks for one of theirs. Or work together. Just let your children be responsible for asking you to work with them if they in turn help you. Raising a responsible child is not always easy. Some children, especially firstborns, seem to accept responsibility more readily. But some, unless you make a concerted effort and have a well-thought-out training program, will continue to resist taking responsibilities. And when their irresponsibility stretches into adulthood, they become a burden to all—even themselves! The greatest gifts you can give your children are the roots of responsibility and the wings of independence.

Chapter 16

Playing Problems Away

You can do anything with children if you only play with them.—Otto Eduard Leopold von Bismarck.

Getting young children to obey can sometimes be a challenge. But it doesn't have to be a chore. If you use a little ingenuity many problems can be "played" away. Children love to play games—even simple ones like "I'll pick up the red blocks and you pick up the blue ones, and let's see who can find the most blocks!" Suddenly the cleanup task becomes a game, frowns turn to smiles, and obedience is fun! Games help to avoid confrontations and to win the child's compliance.

Play-acting is a great way to motivate children to cooperate—especially young children, who enjoy make-believe. For example, when you have to get a brush through a child's tangled hair and you anticipate a battle, play beauty salon. "Good morning, Ms. Adams. I'm so glad you came to my beauty shop. How would you like your hair fixed today? Let's see, I think you would look nice with your hair combed like this . . ." You'll be surprised how much more cooperative a "beauty shop customer" is than a little girl who hates to have Mommy comb her tangled hair.

Have you ever had difficulty getting your child dressed? "Hello, sir. I'm glad you came to my men's store. How would you like a new shirt and pants? I think we have just the thing for you. Please step into this dressing room and try on our bargain for the day."

If your child is running through the house like a fire engine at full speed, say, "Remember, doctor, this is a hospital. The patients are trying to sleep. You will just have to be quiet as you walk down the halls."

When you meet obstinacy head-on, don't buck it; try a role reversal: "You be the mommy and pretend that I'm your little girl. Grab my hand and take me carefully to the other side of the street." Or you might say, "This room is a mess. Pretend that you are my daddy and help me clean my room because you feel sorry that your little girl has to clean it all by herself."

Play restaurant if your child balks at eating dinner. "Here is the food you ordered. It's the specialty of the house. The cook has been busy all afternoon preparing this just for you. And what would you like to drink?" To be really effective, add candlelight and drape a towel over your arm. Eating can become much more interesting when you add a little make-believe.

Maybe your finicky eater would enjoy belonging to the One Bite Club—a special club for anyone willing to sample at least one bite of everything served. Here is how the club got started at the Bennetts' house. Ruth's children were such finicky eaters that the dinner table had become a battleground. Then Grandpa came to visit. He sat halfway through one meal, and that was enough. "What this family needs is a One Bite Club," he announced.

"What's a One Bite Club?" the children asked.

"It's a club in which all the members eat at least one bite of every food that is served. And then, once a week, the club members have a party and go out and play miniature golf."

"When can we go?" the children shouted.

"Not until you sample each food on the table."

"Yuck." They turned up their noses.

"Now, wait," said Grandpa. "It's not that bad. All you have to taste is one bite—and it doesn't have to be a big one."

"This much?" asked one as he held up a half-filled spoon of broccoli.

"Oh, no," said Grandpa. "That's way too much."

Now it was the children's turn to be surprised. The child shook off a little, and with his spoon one fourth filled he asked again if this was enough to join the club.

But once again Grandpa said, "Too much."

Finally there was such a tiny amount on the spoon that the child eagerly put it in his mouth and announced, "I couldn't even taste it."

"Then," said Grandpa nonchalantly, "you might want to take a little more." And without force the child helped himself to a second and bigger bite. That night they celebrated.

You might want to make up some One Bite Club membership cards for your family. Research supports the idea of a One Bite Club. Parents who encourage their children to eat at least one bite of a new food have children with a wider range of food likes than those parents who either force their children to eat everything or don't care what they eat. The One Bite Club is just another game to encourage rather than force compliance.

The One Bite Club might solve the problem of tasting new foods, but what if you want your child to eat everything on the plate? Play the game of guessing how many bites are left. Let each member of the family guess a number, and then the child has to eat everything so you'll know who the winner is. The fun of this game is that the child can decide how much food goes into each bite, controlling the results!

A written message can often be more effective in averting problems than personal involvement. Kari and Kevin were out watering the garden one afternoon, and Kari had the hose. I overheard an argument and a threat about a water fight, so I quickly penned a note. "Dear Kari, please do not water Kevin. He is not a flower. Love, Mommy (from Africa)." I put the note in an envelope and sent it special delivery with Kim. By the time Kari put down the hose and read the note, tempers had cooled and Kevin had escaped to the safety of the house.

Because obedience is such an important lesson for children to learn, we should use every bit of creativity that the Lord has given us to make it easy for children to obey. We want obedience to become a habit. And behavior becomes habitual only if it is repeated often. So instead of forcing children to obey and making the lesson distasteful, why not play-act problems away and make the obedience lesson not only effective but fun?

You can use fun to break habits. Do you have a little Linus walking around your house with a pacifier in his mouth and a threadbare, nondescript rag trailing around behind? Most children have a difficult time giving up these comfort devices. When Mom or Dad decides the security crutch has to go, the result is too often a tug-of-war.

But there is another way if you're a game-playing parent. You must first realize that there's nothing wrong when infants and young children have pacifiers, security blankets, and special toys. So don't rush a reluctant child into prematurely giving these up. But when you feel it's time for your child to move on to more grown-up behavior, you might want to try the habit-breaking game Raylene played with Shawnee.

Shawnee was 2½ years old and still very dependent on her special satiny blanket. She also needed her pacifier to go to sleep. Raylene didn't have a problem with the blanket, but the pacifier was beginning to be a nuisance, and she suspected that it should no longer be necessary.

Dreading the inevitable trauma this transition would cause, she kept putting it off until one day when she ran into a friend who also had a little girl about Shawnee's age. And they had a new puppy with them! After appropriate admiration was expressed, little Beth announced, "I traded my bottle for the puppy."

"What's this?" Raylene asked. Her interest sparked.

"Oh," said Beth's mother, "Beth was so attached to her bottle that any attempt to take it away was met with tears and pleading to have it back. Since she had her heart set on getting a puppy, we got the idea that she could get the puppy by trading her bottle for it. And you know, it worked! Since she now has something she very much wanted, and since it was her own decision, I didn't come off looking like the big bad mommy. And she has no reason to beg and plead for her bottle anymore."

"What a marvelous idea," Raylene exclaimed. "I'm going to try it with Shawnee's pacifier."

Shawnee wanted a doll carriage, so Raylene suggested that Shawnee trade her pacifier for one. Shawnee thought about the possibility for a couple of days and finally decided it was worth it. At last the time came for the transaction. Mom made all the arrangements so the clerk would not be too startled when a very solemn 2½-year-old handed the clerk her precious pacifier. With shining eyes Shawnee proudly placed her baby doll into the carriage and wheeled it out of the store.

So if you find yourself wishing your little Linus would give up his bottle, blanket, or pacifier, why not wait until he wants something badly enough to be willing to trade for it? If it worked with Beth and Shawnee, chances are it will work for your little one, too.

You can also use games to help out at bathtime. I've received a number of letters from parents telling about the fun things they have done to get their little ones to take a bath. Some of these are so clever I think they're worth sharing.

First, try coloring the bathwater; chances are your child will want to hop in. Just add several drops of food coloring to the water. If it's made to be put into our bodies, it certainly won't hurt the outside. Chances are your child will watch wide-eyed as the color swirls and is gradually diluted with the water. The father who gave me this idea used red food coloring and told the story of Moses in Egypt when the sea turned red like blood. His child was fascinated. You could also use two colors at once and make bathtime a lesson about primary and secondary colors. But limit the colors to two unless you like the look of muddy water.

Another idea is to finger-paint on the walls of the shower—just don't use regular finger paint! Instead, put a lot of Ivory Soap flakes in a little warm water and whip it up with an electric beater until it's like whipped cream. You can add a little food coloring if you want. Be sure to have a rubber mat on the shower floor so your child won't slip. Then when your child is finished, just turn on the shower or take a big sponge and wash everything off. The shower and the child will both be cleaned in the process.

Bathtub time is always more fun when you have some bath toys to play with, but many moms and dads complain of having bath toys all over the tub or bathroom floor. If this is a problem in your home, give your children a fishnet and challenge them to capture all the floating toys before the water drains away. Then the toys can be kept in the fishnet to drip-dry in the tub. You can either leave them in the tub until the next bathtime, or put the toy-filled net away under the sink or in a closet.

Why not turn that bathtub into a lake of sailboats? It won't cost a thing, because children can make these boats all by themselves. Just take half a walnut shell, chew a little bubble gum, stick it inside the shell, and put a toothpick into the gum for the mast. Then cut out little squares of cloth for the sails, and you can have a fleet of boats in no time. Actually, anything that floats can make a boat: jar lids placed upside-down, pieces of wood, paper cups.

One dad combined bathtub time with storytelling time. His children loved hearing all the stories about when he was a boy—and even Bible stories took on new meaning the way Dad told them. Finally, one parent suggested that you gather some objects from the house and ask your child to sort them into things that float and things that sink. Bathtime can be an important learning time, and with a little creativity it may become a highlight in your child's life.

But in some families it's bedtime, not bathtime, that's a big problem. If you've found bedtime is bedlam time, maybe it's time for a game.

I'll never forget the mother who told me she had tried everything, and still her children resisted the idea of putting on their pajamas and getting into bed. Suddenly, inspiration hit! "Hurry," she called, "I've got a prize for the first kid in bed wearing someone else's pajamas!" You should have seen those children trade pajamas—like their lives depended on it—and before you knew it, they were in bed. Then, of course, everyone looked so funny dressed in PJs that didn't fit that Mom made them get back out of bed while she took a picture.

If you have young children who don't seem to respond to your request to go to bed, you might get more compliance if you offer them an animal ride to bed. During the preschool years our kids were carried to bed on monkeys, giraffes, ostriches, and even sharks. They loved it.

My friend Elmar came up with an innovative bedtime game to solve a problem he was having with his son, Chad. During the first three years of Chad's life, Elmar was a superbusy medical student and resident. Time was not his own; he practically lived at the hospital while his wife, Darilee, took the major responsibility for caring for the kids.

With those years of training over and a practice established, Elmar decided he wanted to spend more time with his son. He especially wanted to be the one to put Chad to bed, read him a story, say prayers with him, and tuck him in with a hug and kiss.

But Chad would have nothing to do with this. When well-meaning Dad tried, Chad cried for his mommy. So Darilee came and tucked Chad into bed. Elmar decided he wasn't going to take no for an answer. He devised the following strategy. When Darilee started to tuck Chad into bed, Elmar quietly crept into the bedroom on his hands and knees. Because of the way the crib was situated, Chad could not see anyone entering the room. Then Elmar picked up a small rubber ball and tossed it over the end of the bed, where it landed on Chad's pillow.

Chad, of course, was surprised. But he did what any normal 3-year-old would do—he picked it up and tossed it back outside the crib. Elmar caught it and tossed it again. Chad was intrigued with the game. Back and forth the ball went, accompanied by Chad's squeals of delight. Finally, Daddy popped into sight, hugged and kissed Chad, whispered a good-night prayer, and tucked him into bed.

The next evening Chad said to his mother, "Mommy, I want Daddy to put me to bed just like he did last night." So Mom put Chad into bed while Elmar crept in quietly and tossed a soft toy into the crib. Back and forth it went, until Elmar popped up and hugged and kissed his son. This became the bedtime ritual.

A couple weeks later the family was entertaining a guest. Just about bedtime the guest asked Chad if his dad ever read stories to him at bedtime. "No," said Chad with a gleam in his eye. "He just throws things at me!"

If a happy bedtime means throwing things when other parents are reading bedtime stories, why not? With a little creativity you can both be winners.

One of the main goals of easy obedience is that of encouraging self-discipline, and I've found that games have been extremely effective in that area. For example, when Kevin was younger he rarely left for school with a clean face until we stopped giving commands and started playing a game: "Whoever walks outside the house with a dirty face gets to empty the wastebaskets." (Of course, that is a game of imposed consequences. But we acted as though we were playing a game rather than disciplining.) Soon I was having a hard time finding anyone to empty the trash—but faces were clean. Nine thousand, three hundred forty-two reminders did not get through to Kevin, but one simple game made the difference.

When you initiate a game to teach your child responsibility, it's important that the rules apply to the entire family. Our family uses an electric toothbrush, and for years Jan and Kevin were constantly reminding me to take my toothbrush off the appliance when I was finished. Kevin finally decided that the family should play this game: "Whoever forgets to take the toothbrush off has to go to their bedroom and count to 25." Wouldn't you know, Kevin was the first one who had to count to 25! But the game also helped me to remember this simple task.

If you decide to try this technique, make sure that every family member agrees to play and has a say in setting the rules. Games lose their value if they cease to be fun or if the consequences of losing are not consistently carried out.

If you're trying to teach your children to be thorough when doing a task, you might want to try variations of the next two games.

Why not hide pennies under various items where the children need to dust? If you don't expect the item to be picked up and dusted under, then leave the penny partially visible. Tell your children how many you've hidden and see if they can find them all.

One mom paid her child a quarter for sweeping the leaves off the patio, but asked for a penny back for every leaf that was left when the job was finished. She didn't get anything back!

Playing make-believe can also be an effective way to help children discipline themselves. Sue was the mom of two preschoolers who seemed to pick up every dirty word, unkind behavior, or moody characteristic they ever observed. And there were some neighborhood kids who exhibited a lot of what was, to her, unacceptable behavior. What should she do? Keep her children home all day, away from bad influences?

She tried keeping them home, but her children were miserable. They wanted to play with friends. After a couple days at home, they felt like prisoners—and she like a jailer. That was no way to live. So she changed her attack.

First, she focused on making their backyard into a children's paradise. She ordered a truckload of sand for a giant sandpile and purchased water hoses, buckets, shovels, plastic trucks, and other sand toys. Before she knew it, word had spread through the neighborhood.

But whenever a child came to play or was caught sneaking over the back fence, Sue would say, "You may play here, but I'm the ruler of this domain, and you'll have to obey my rules, or you'll get kicked out and can't come back for two days." Then she very carefully showed them the boundary of her realm—where the fence line was—and explained the rules.

Rule number one: No bad words. No swearing or taking God's name in vain. She gave them examples of words that she had heard the neighborhood children say that were unacceptable, so they knew without a shadow of a doubt what was expected.

The second law in her land was the golden rule: "Treat others as you want others to treat you."

Sue made herself a crown to wear to remind the children that they were guests in her dominion. The result was unbelievable. Children she had heard previously arguing and calling each other names were playing side by side in perfect harmony.

One time the bully of the neighborhood tested the rules. He got mad, threw sand, and shouted obscenities at a friend who had accidentally stepped on the road he was building.

Sue plopped on her crown and gently but firmly escorted the offending child off their property. She explained very carefully that he was banished for two days. She then called his mother so she'd know why he'd been sent home. After that, no one challenged the rules.

Why do games like these motivate self-discipline? Games take the work out of doing what you have to do. Children set on being stubbornly resistant suddenly become captivated by the challenge of the game. Before they know it they are having a good time obeying. Since children love to play games, what a great incentive they have to be self-disciplined enough to be able to participate.

I once read that if parents would play more with their children, their children would love and respect them more—more than if they were always serious and acted their age. This is true because children love playful people. Children establish close ties with people who they sense enjoy being with them. And if they have this relationship with their folks and other authority figures, they won't resent an occasional correction when it needs to be made.

I didn't have any trouble playing with my preschoolers. I wore the skin off my knees creeping around the floor playing piggyback, and I found every secret hiding place in our yard playing hide-and-seek. I've enjoyed pitching balls to Kevin, although I didn't do it as often as he wished. Young children love to play with their parents, but teens enjoy playful parents too.

I was intrigued by the story Gloria Gaither tells about her playful mother. She had a slumber party one night, and when it got fairly late her mother called up to them, "All right, girls. It's time to go to sleep."

The firmness of her voice meant business, so they turned off the light and crawled into bed. They were trying their best to get to sleep when they felt water sprinkling on their faces. They finally figured out it was coming in through the bedroom window. They ran to the window to investigate, and there was Mom in her robe and slippers with the water hose.

That was too much! The girls raced downstairs to get back at her. As they ran through the kitchen, they were surprised to find a huge pan of popcorn waiting for them. Then they all sat down to enjoy the midnight snack while Mom told them ghost stories in the dark. Gloria fondly remembers the night when her mom forgot to act her age.

Moms and dads can be a lot of fun. But too often we get caught up in everything we need to do and forget to laugh. It's been so long since we've been kids, we've forgotten how to act silly, play jokes, and be a child among our children. And I'm speaking for myself.

One day my daughter said to me, "Mom, I wish you were more like Sherry's mother. She's so much fun to be with. We can tell her anything, and she just laughs with us like another teenager. She never lectures us—even though I know she'd correct us if we needed it."

Well, I want to be fun too. And I can, if I just determine not to take life so seriously. Occasionally I need to step off my parental pedestal and forget about all my weighty adult responsibilities. I need to take a deep breath, let down my hair, put on my grubbies, and play with the children God gave me.

After all, King Solomon says, "Everything is appropriate in its own time. . . . So I conclude that, first, there is nothing better for a man than to be happy and to enjoy himself as long as he can; and second, that he should eat and drink and enjoy the fruits of his labors, for these are gifts from God" (Eccl. 3:11-13, TLB).

Aren't your children the most precious gifts of all? Why not play problems away if at all possible? When you do, you'll find yourself enjoying your child and your job as a creative disciplinarian twice as much, and you'll find that obedience comes easier too.

Chapter 17

Teaching Values Early

Children are unpredictable. You never know what inconsistency they're going to catch you in next.—Franklin P. Jones.

Many of the behaviors you like or dislike in your child directly reflect what you value. For example, there's really nothing wrong with your children eating with their fingers, if their fingers are clean. Whether children should use fingers or a fork is dictated by values. How important is it to you that your children abide by culturally accepted norms? Other areas of behavior that reflect values might include the following:

1. *Religious behavior,* such as saying the blessing before eating, or not misusing the name of God.
2. *Social behavior,* such as standing when you are introduced to a person who is standing, or not interrupting adults who are talking.
3. *Recreational activities.* Going to movies or listening to rock music may be right or wrong, depending upon your values. Other parents object to recreational hunting, or playing with war toys.
4. *Health behavior,* such as going to sleep at a regular time, avoiding junk foods, and not eating between meals, may reflect individual values.
5. *Acceptable appearance has to do with values.* Some parents insist that their children wear suits and ties to church. Others disapprove of new hairstyles or false eyelashes. Some have a hang-up about wearing stripes and plaids together!
6. *Behavior and attitudes about school* may also reflect values. It's not morally wrong to get C's or D's in school, nor will low grades always hurt a child, but the way some parents react, you would think it was the end of the world!

The majority of corrections that parents impose on their children are a direct reflection of their own values. These are behaviors the parent feels strongly about, not because these behaviors hurt the individual, others, or things, but because they're something they value personally.

Parental values differ. You and your spouse may not agree on such things as the importance of maintaining a vegetarian diet, the significance of getting to bed at a decent hour, or how much time a child needs for free play. These value clashes can cause major conflicts, leaving the child uncertain about what is really important.

It's also true that certain behavior may be tolerated in one household and strictly forbidden in another. Since there is nothing inherently right or wrong in these behaviors, it can lead to severe parent-child conflicts, because children can't understand why their friends get away with behavior that is strictly forbidden for them.

The way to minimize these conflicts as much as possible is to clearly establish what is acceptable value-related behavior and to do it as early in life as possible—preferably during infancy. Then when you hear "But Jimmy gets to do that. Why can't I?" you have an answer. If you have clearly established acceptable behavior for your family, you can say, "This is something that the Kuzma family feels is important." Or "Our family's values are different, and we couldn't allow that." You may also say, "Because I feel so strongly about that, I can't let you do it—it would hurt me if you did."

When a value clash occurs with older children who will make their own decisions regardless of your values, you may have to say, "What you want to do conflicts with my value system. But you are now old enough to establish your own values." Then after explaining the reason you value what you do, you might say, "I hope you will carefully consider why I value what I do before making your decision."

One of the best ways for young children to "catch" your values is to let them hear you expressing them—within their hearing but not directed toward them. Often a conversation overheard will have more impact than words spoken specifically to them.

The chances are slim that your children will grow up with exactly the same values as yours. They may be similar, but even slight differences in the area of values can cause conflict. Wise parents understand this and won't force their own values on their children. Only two options remain: to teach by precept and to teach by example.

To teach by precept (instruction) means to admonish or to influence your child from an early age according to a basic standard of conduct. In addition, you should present information and encourage unemotional discussions about the rationale behind your values.

To teach by example, you must consistently live by your values. You cannot have one set of values that you try to impose on your children while you live by another.

When Lily's daughter, Maria, was just 6 she became enthralled by the gaudy jewelry, excessive makeup, and long, painted artificial fingernails she observed on others. Television added fuel to the fire of her desire to "look beautiful." The problem was that Lily's value system was very different. She believed in a simple, modest, unpretentious look. She believed in natural beauty—being physically fit, having healthy skin, wearing only a little makeup and almost no jewelry. Of course, she wanted Maria to feel the same way.

Lily was really worried. If Maria had such a strong desire for artificial "beauty" at age 6, what would she be like at 16, with the weird hairstyles and immodest fashions that might well be in vogue?

Wisely Lily recognized that to forbid certain things strictly might make them more enticing to her youngster, until obtaining the forbidden became the burning desire. She certainly didn't want that. Lily hoped that once Maria's curiosity was satisfied, the fancy would pass.

Lily approached the issue by saying, "It's fun to look pretty. God loves beauty too. That's why He made us just the way we are. But God says that what is on the inside is really the most important. He wants you to have a beautiful personality, to be friendly and kind.

"Sometimes people think they can get more attention by putting on gaudy jewelry and wearing brightly colored makeup and long, artificial fingernails. I don't think this is necessary. I believe in modesty and simplicity. If you would like to dress up and pretend you are a fancy lady, like the ones you see on TV, then I'll help you. But when you go outside our home, to school or to church, I want people to see God's beautiful creation—the real you—and not just store-bought jewelry and colored paint on your face and nails. OK?" (Lily also didn't want Maria to be rewarded by having others give her a lot of attention when wearing these things.)

That has worked with Maria—at least for now. If the issue surfaces again, Lily might have to say, "Maria, there are many people you can look to in this world as an example of what is an appropriate appearance. I would be happy if you'd follow my example. You can wear as much makeup, colored nail polish, and jewelry as I wear. Or you might enjoy taking a beauty and poise class, in which you can learn to apply makeup and accessories in such a way as to enhance your God-given beauty and not detract from it. Plus, I believe that wearing the proper colors that complement your skin tones and having the right hairstyle for your face have much more to do with being attractive than wearing excessive makeup and jewelry. Would you like to have a professional help you in these areas?"

This approach may resolve the value conflict—at least for a while. But what should Lily do when Maria is 16 and insists she wants to wear a wild hairstyle or short skirts and see-through blouses?

The answer depends on the strength of Lily's values. Some mothers might feel that by 16 years of age a girl should be able to make choices about her personal appearance. Others would take a stronger stand. "No, I'm sorry, I cannot let you wear immodest styles or styles that represent values very different from our own. Our family believes in simplicity and modesty—and one way we have lived that value is in appearance. This is so important to me, that I must take a strong stand and say no. I hope you will understand."

But what if she doesn't? What if this continues to be an issue? The resolution of this value conflict will be determined by four things:

1. How firmly this value has been established in early childhood—through both precept and example.
2. The reasonableness of the value. Does it make sense?
3. The quality of the rapport between parent and child.
4. The influence of significant peers.

If Maria loves her mother and doesn't want to hurt her, this will influence her decision, regardless of peer pressure. But if Maria is rebelling and doesn't care about her mother's feelings, or if she intentionally wants to hurt her mother, then watch out!

You cannot dictate what values your children will ultimately hold. But if you want them to respect your values and if you want to increase the chances of their living by them during their growing years, then in addition to maintaining a good relationship with your children, be sure your values are reasonable, that you establish them early, and that you consistently maintain them through instruction and example.

What values are you teaching through your example? Charles was a sensitive and kind father. But something happened to him when he got behind the wheel. He hated to waste time on the road, so sometimes his priorities got a little mixed up. One time he and his family were driving back home after a long holiday weekend. Traffic was bad, and when he was forced to drop below 55 mph he became agitated and began to change lanes to get past some of the slower cars—all the time complaining about the other drivers on the road who were causing this mess.

During one such move his car came within a few feet of a truck's rear bumper, and he stayed there, waiting to pass. Once he passed, he noticed the same truck directly behind him. He thought nothing of it until the truck moved up to within a few inches of his bumper.

Realizing he was getting some of his own medicine, he went along with it for a while, but then he grew angry and tried an old trick of the road—tapping the brake pedal so that the brake lights came on but the car didn't slow down much.

It worked magnificently. Frightened by his apparent braking, the driver of the truck jammed on his brakes, producing a short, swerving skid. All this time, the children in the back seat were observing and pleading, "Daddy, don't!"

But the game had just begun. The truck moved up again, then went into the adjoining lane and pulled up beside Charles's car. The driver lowered the window. Charles saw the irate face of his opponent and expected a brief shouting match, but instead found himself looking down the barrel of a shotgun.

Enough was enough. Charles slowed down. The driver of the truck passed, pulled in front of Charles, and then slammed on his brakes to reduce his speed—and Charles's—to less than 10 mph. Behind them, the sound of screeching brakes registered the effects of the duel.

Afterward, Charles was ashamed of himself. He felt especially bad that his children had witnessed his childish behavior. He certainly didn't want them driving like that someday. So he admitted that he'd been wrong and asked his children to forgive him. They talked about the importance of being a good witness on the road and how driving by the golden rule is just as important as living by the golden rule. If nothing else, it would keep them all a lot safer!

Charles had not been a good example for his children. Without his apology and correction, they might have ended up imitating his behavior and the values it represented.

It's easy to get discouraged when you see your children picking up the very things you dislike most about yourself. But take courage—they also pick up the positive. After lamenting the bad habits my children had picked up from me, I was encouraged one day when I found my girls picking up a positive value. They were 6 and 8 years of age, respectively, and just learning to keep their room clean.

"Girls, make your beds and pick up your clothing before we leave," I shouted above the hustle and bustle of an early-morning departure. I had 30 minutes' worth of things to do and about half that time to do them in, so I was too rushed to supervise the cleanup operation I had requested.

Five minutes before departure time I gave the last instruction, "Get into the car. We're leaving." They promptly obeyed as I grabbed my coat and purse from the bedroom and started down the hall. As I passed the girls' room I glanced in to make sure everything was organized for the day.

"Oh, no," I sighed. Their room was a mess. Nothing had been done. Impulsively I started to yell at them to come back and make their beds, but I stopped myself. After all, it was partly my fault for not supervising them more closely—and they were already in the car. Rather than get everyone upset, why not handle the situation with a little creativity and teach them the value of serving others?

I put down my purse and coat, picked up their clothing, and then quickly made their beds. The room looked presentable. Then I took a large piece of paper and wrote, "Dear Kim and Kari, I made your beds because I love you. Love, Mommy." I pinned the note to the top bunk bedspread, where it was sure to be seen, and then got into the car without saying anything to the girls about what I had done.

When we returned home Kim and Kari went to their room. I listened for their discovery. They seemed not to notice that their room was in order, but they immediately spied the note.

"What does it say?" asked Kari. Kim went over to the note, unpinned it, and read it to Kari.

"Hey, Mom did clean up!" exclaimed Kari as she glanced back at the beds.

"Yeah," said Kim. "Mommy sure must love us."

I waited for them to come running out and thank me—but like the nine lepers who were healed by Jesus, they never did. *Well,* I thought, *that surely didn't have the effect I hoped it would,* and I forgot about the situation.

About three weeks later I was again checking the girls' room. This time everything was in order. Then I noticed a note pinned onto Kari's bedspread. I bent down and read it. "Dear Kari, I made your bed because I love you. Love, Kim."

This time it was my turn to be surprised! Children follow good examples as well as bad. So take heart, parents. Continue being the kind of example you know Christ would want you to be. And don't be surprised when your values rub off on your children.

Chapter 18

Age-related Problems of Young Children

The fastest road to furthering independence in your children is total attention to the needs of your children in their dependent years.—Herbert Ratner.

Much of a young child's inappropriate behavior is age-related. In other words, the behavior is really not inappropriate or it can be explained, if you consider the child's stage of development. Knowing this helps parents become more understanding disciplinarians. This chapter will attempt to answer some of those age-related questions that parents have concerning their children.

The previous chapters have described the principles of easy obedience. It's now time to take those principles and make them practical. I've been answering parents' questions for years in my syndicated Dr. Kay's Q & A column. Here's how easy obedience can solve 13 child-rearing problems that you may have with your young children.

- Obnoxious behavior
- Name-calling
- Overcoming fear
- Sibling rivalry
- Toilet training
- Routines
- Rubbish talk
- Biting
- Hyperactivity
- Whining
- Premature sexual behavior
- Tattling
- Cleaning rooms

Obnoxious behavior

Question: Why is it that my children insist on doing the very things that upset me the most? For example, bathroom talk and four-letter words in front of company, or whining when I'm trying to get dinner ready, or teasing each other when I'm on the phone. These things really get my goat!

Answer: One of the fundamental laws of parenthood is If children know what gets your goat, they'll get it. It's not that they want to persecute you. Neither are they out looking for things you don't like. For the most part, children enjoy pleasing adults. But at times children misbehave to get your attention, to win a power struggle, or just to reap the sweet taste of revenge. When children know what really upsets you, it gives them ammunition to get back at you when they're angry.

Typical "goat-getting" behaviors usually are things parents have very little control over, such as saying "dirty" words, whining, lying, sassing, being lazy, or misbehaving when you are too involved to take action. Undue attention to these behaviors is rewarding, and it's exactly what a child wants.

Therefore, react in a calm, matter-of-fact way. Be firm. Explain the reason the behavior is forbidden and let them know the consequences of a repeat performance. Then move on. Don't dwell on the misbehavior. In other words, don't let them know what really gets your goat!

Name-calling

Question: Should I intervene when my 5-year-old calls her younger brother names such as "stupid"?

Answer: Yes. Family loyalty is important. Siblings should not be allowed to treat each other in ways that are demeaning or that cause one's self-worth to be destroyed. Instead, they should be encouraged to support and help each other as much as possible.

Calling each other names is often a beginning sign of sibling rivalry. Carefully analyze your family's interactions to determine what might be causing this rivalry. There could be some underlying jealousy that needs to be healed before the name-calling will go away. Check at the library for children's books on jealousy. A story is a great way to introduce the topic and ask your daughter how she feels. You might get some valuable insights into what you're doing that may contribute to these jealousy feelings.

Children, especially young ones, take names seriously. If your son hears a negative term such as "stupid" often enough, it becomes like a negative script that can affect his life.

Calling people names can also be a bad habit. That's why this behavior should be stopped immediately. Calmly say, "You may not hurt another person, and calling people names hurts their feelings. If you children can't get along together, I will have to separate you."

But don't make a federal case out of your daughter's name-calling. If she knows this really disturbs you, she has a powerful weapon she can use anytime she is angry at you. And guess who may be called a bad name next!

Children pick up name-calling from TV, friends, and occasionally from parents who mutter "stupid" when someone cuts in front of them on the freeway. To retrain the entire family to see people in the most positive light possible, you might play the game in which if someone calls someone else a bad word, they have to say immediately three positive things about that person. It can be fun—and educational, too.

Overcoming fear

Question: I've got 2-year-old twins who are abnormally fearful, especially about being bitten. We can't go to a park where there might be a dog, or even to Chuck E. Cheese's, without our boys screaming. I've never seen kids like this. People have asked us what we've done to them to make them so fearful. Please help me.

Answer: Children 2 years of age fear the unknown and not being able to control their environment. Sudden movements of animals are particularly frightening. Plus, you've got double trouble, because fear is contagious. When one is scared, the other gets frightened, which makes the fear of the first even worse! It may make you feel better to know that bright children are often the most frightened at a young age because they can perceive the dangers in a situation and also are smart enough to know they don't have the skills to cope.

Your children's fears are real to them, whether or not they are reasonable. You must accept that fact and talk about their fears without ridicule. Respect your boys' feelings, and don't take them into situations that you know will upset them. They will grow out of these fears in their own time as they begin to associate the objects they fear with pleasant situations.

Start your reprogramming project by making sure the boys feel as secure as possible in their home environment. Don't rush them to Chuck E. Cheese's and other places of entertainment. In time they will be begging you to do this and will be in the middle of the petting zoo. Just let them decide when they're ready, and don't judge your boys by what other children their age are doing.

When you venture to a new place, stay close to them. Hold them in your arms if possible. Don't put them down unless they want down. Children are fearful in new situations when they don't know whether or not they can trust their parents, and the result is to hold on tighter, or scream louder to try to get you to understand.

Bring small, slow-moving animals into your house as pets. Start with caterpillars, then graduate to something like a guinea pig in a cage, but don't force your boys to touch it. They will in their own time, when they see you having fun handling it. A grown cat who doesn't mind being handled and is declawed makes a good starter pet, but remember, 2-year-olds can be rather rough with small animals, so don't rush into this experience.

As your boys grow, become more secure in new environments, and have positive experiences with animals, their fears will subside.

Sibling rivalry

Question: My 3-year-old and almost-2-year-old are constantly fighting. They will sometimes fight over the same toy, even though there's another one just like it that one could have! I can't stand the constant bickering. I've tried separating them. I've tried warning them I'll take the fought-over toy and put it up—and I've done it. I've tried sitting them in chairs and telling them they can't play together until they can play nicely. But nothing seems to work.

Answer: The reason nothing works has something to do with their age. Toddlers and preschoolers are egocentric. That means that no matter how much effort you put into explaining that sharing is a virtue, or why it's better to say please than grab things from the other, they have a hard time understanding that others have rights. Their own self or ego is of primary importance. They think the world revolves around themselves. If they want something, they should have it. If it's in their hand, it's theirs. Period.

All your lecturing, separating, and threatening do little good. Children grow out of egocentricity by experiencing consequences, receiving simple instruction of how to get what they want without fighting, *and by maturing*. But it doesn't happen overnight. So even though I'm going to give you a few pointers, don't expect miracles!

Here's the question you're going to want to teach your children to ask each other: "When you're finished, may I have the toy?" It's a great question, because it should always get a yes. You're going to have to explain that when they are finished, they don't want the toy anymore, and therefore they shouldn't care if the other plays with it. That's why they answer that question yes.

Then when the toy is laid aside, you must remind the child to tell the other that he or she can now use the toy. This interaction rewards both. It rewards the first child with a yes response and the good feeling of doing something nice for the other. And it rewards the second child with finally getting the toy.

Notice how the fighting begins. If there's a certain pattern, such as one child always grabbing the toy from the other, can you think of ways to divert the tug-of-war before it becomes World War III? Prevention is always the best cure!

Watch from the sidelines to make sure there's no dirty play—such as hair-pulling and biting. When that happens, it's "time-out." "If you can't play together nicely, you'll have to play alone."

And finally, don't jump into every squabble. A certain amount of fighting seems to be necessary for children to learn problem-solving skills. I remember from graduate school days a study that suggested children had to go through a certain amount of conflict to learn the natural consequences of their antisocial behavior. Basically, the nursery school children who had enough teachers to help them handle conflicts ended up fighting more in kindergarten than children who didn't have the "advantage" of intervening nursery school teachers.

Hang in there, Mom. The squabbling years may be just a necessary part of your children's social education. Just pray they're quick learners!

Toilet training

Question: My son is almost 3½, and he's not toilet trained yet. He is very strong-willed, and I feel he is resisting just because he knows it would make me happy if he would do it. This has become a problem at this time, because he was looking forward to starting preschool, but I know they won't take him if he isn't trained.

Answer: Many 3- and 4-year-olds aren't yet toilet trained—and it's not uncommon for 6- and 7-year-olds to get so involved in activities that they can't make it to the toilet in time. At times of stress or excitement, school-aged children sometimes have accidents. Your child may be a late bloomer when it comes to bladder and bowel control. So lighten up!

A child who is ready physically to be toilet trained may need just a little regularity and psychological motivation. Preschool may be your answer. Some preschools will take children who could use the toilet but won't, and will work with them for a trial period, especially if the child really wants to attend. The teacher usually asks Mom to send a number of changes of clothing. When an accident occurs, the teacher lets a child wash himself and the dirty underwear. With a teacher who encourages a child with an "I can" attitude, combined with peer pressure and the desire to attend preschool, it usually doesn't take a child long to train himself.

But if you're not lucky enough to find such a teacher, and if your son's resistance is basically a struggle for power, then you're going to have to transfer the responsibility for toileting behavior back on his shoulders. Tell him something like this: "You know that big people urinate and have bowel movements in the toilet. Mommy has been pushing you to use the toilet. But that's not really Mommy's responsibility. It's your responsibility to decide when you want to use the toilet. During the day you can choose whether or not you would like to wear a diaper or underpants. But if you soil them, you will need to clean yourself up. I will help you if you ask me. If you choose to stay in dirty diapers, or if you don't clean a bowel movement off your bottom, it could make your skin hurt. That is one of the consequences of not using the toilet. Also, other people don't like to smell dirty diapers, so your friends may not want to play with you if you smell—or they might tease you. I might even ask you to go into another room if the smell bothers me."

I know this is a whopper of a speech for a preschooler. You will have to say it over and over. And it's going to be very hard for you not to be constantly reminding your son. Instead, when he's playing you might say something like "When you're having so much fun, I know it's sometimes hard to remember to use the toilet, so if you want me to remind you, just let me know."

When he has an accident, you're going to have to be very calm and remind him that he had the choice. He could have either gone in the toilet and had the fun of flushing it, or he could have gone in his pants and cleaned himself up.

Eventually, age and peer pressure are going to win out—and your son will decide that the toilet was a great invention!

Routines

Question: I'm a recently divorced mom with a job that has irregular hours. I sometimes pick up my 2- and 4-year-old daughters from day care at 6:00 p.m., and other nights as late as 8:30. By the time we get home and eat, I'm ready for bed, but I can't get them to settle down. If they don't get their sleep, they throw a fit when I get them up and try to dress them in the morning.

Answer: Children need the security that routine and regularity bring. Because of the divorce, your children have experienced a lot of change. They appear to be holding on to you as if you too may be going to leave them. Even going to sleep may be threatening to them, because they don't really know if you'll be there in the morning. Then when they wake up, they are facing separation from you once again as you take them off to day care. They need a lot of reassurance.

It is very disturbing to children in day care when their parents pick them up at irregular times. Children feel more secure within a routine. Preschoolers tell the time of day not by a clock, but by the routines in their lives. They determine the time you will pick them up from day care in the same way. For example, after nap, juice, a story, and outside play, their parents come. If the pickup time is irregular, this can be very disturbing. Even children with very secure families can become frightened when other children are being picked up and their parents are late.

Sometimes when children feel insecure, they try to control their world, feeling that if they are in control at least they know what to expect. This may be another reason your children are putting up such a fuss about bedtime and wake-up time. It is the only time of the day you are with them. If they can control the situation, perhaps they can put off having to separate from you by going to bed, or by having to go to day care. And in addition, they can get more of your attention, which they crave so much.

Here's a suggestion: Seriously consider how you can make life more regular for your children. Don't say it is impossible. Say it *is* possible and then figure out how! There are always options. Every problem has a solution, or it wouldn't be a problem—it would be reality!

Next, establish a bedtime routine. About one hour after supper, play pickup, give them a bath (that relaxes children), and read them two or three stories. (*No* TV—not even during supper!) Say prayers. Rub their backs for five minutes, say good-night, and leave. If one has an especially hard time falling asleep, tell her in private that if she hasn't fallen asleep by the time the other falls asleep, she can get up and play quietly for another 15 minutes. This promise will keep her as quiet as possible so the other will go to sleep quickly. Chances are she will seldom exercise this option, as she too will fall asleep!

Rubbish talk

Question: I have a 4½-year-old boy who is going through a phase of "rubbish" talk! This gibberish goes on nonstop, and I'm about to go crazy. I've withheld privileges, threatened, and sent him to his room, but it doesn't seem to be getting any better.

Answer: Rubbish talk is exactly what you say it is—a phase. There may be a few things you can do to make yourself a little more comfortable while it lasts, such as wearing earplugs, turning up the volume of the radio, and walking out of the room. But like chicken pox, it will most likely have to run its course before it disappears. And, like chicken pox, the more you scratch or try to get rid of this behavior, the more likely it will leave some scars of hard feelings between the two of you.

There are two reasons preschoolers talk gibberish, nonsense, and sometimes risqué or "bathroom" talk. The first has to do with their stage of language development. Although a person's vocabulary continues to increase throughout most of life, by 5 years of age a child has mastered all the major rules for sentence structure and may have a speaking vocabulary of 2,000 or 3,000 words. With the hard work of mastering basic communication skills behind him, your son is now ready to use his language in creative ways. He becomes fascinated with words, playing with them, letting them roll off his tongue, and creating interesting sounds and combinations.

Instead of punishing your child for what you call rubbish, celebrate his incredible achievement. Say, "It's fun to play with words, isn't it? If you want me to understand, you're going to have to tell me in words I know." Or play his game and jabber gibberish back. Enjoy this stage!

The second reason for the nonstop rubbish talk is that it's likely gotten him a great deal of attention. Children enjoy the shock value that risqué or nonsense words have on others. And because attention is rewarding, the more attention you give, the longer it will last. So instead of trying to inhibit the talk, provide a means to get it out without it frustrating you to the point that you end up threatening or punishing. Give him a tape recorder. Set up a recording "studio" in his room or a place where you can't hear it, and let him jabber to his heart's content. And guess what? Even he will grow tired of it!

When you don't think you can stand your child's age-related behavior, ask yourself, "If I knew I had to endure this just for today, and tomorrow it would be over, would I be able to live with it?" If yes, remember, you have been asked to live only a day at a time. Don't worry about tomorrow. Wake up each morning with the attitude "I have to put up with this only today. I can do that." If you begin thinking, *This rubbish talk may last six months*, you'll go crazy—not because of the behavior right now, but because of your worry that it will never end! But take heart, this too shall pass!

Biting

Question: My 2-year-old bites when he doesn't get what he wants. I don't know how to stop it! My friends told me to bite him back. I've tried, but it hasn't worked. Should I just keep this up, or is there a better way?

Answer: Let me explain why biting back works for some children, and why you should not continue biting your child. I'm one of those parents who had a child who was cured from his biting by getting bitten in return. Kevin was over at my sister's house. He bit his little cousin, and Joanie grabbed him and bit him back, and he never did it again! Why did it work? It was the shock factor. He didn't expect it.

Shock therapy, in various forms, gets the child's attention, helps him refocus, and frightens him enough to try to avoid getting the shock again. Surprise is the basic element of success. Once you take the surprise element out of what you do, and the child expects it as a consequence, it is no longer effective. Spanking, throwing cold water on a child, ignoring, slapping hands, or a loud scream are all shock therapy techniques. The danger is that these methods, when overused, can become abusive and end up causing the child to become hostile and rebellious.

Let me give an example: parents tell success stories of stopping temper tantrums in children by throwing a pitcher of cold water at them. Can you imagine how ridiculous it would be to throw cold water for every misbehavior? It might work once or even twice, but that's it! Yet many parents continue to use shock techniques over and over, even if they cease to be effective.

Why don't parenting classes teach shock techniques? Because parents do these things automatically and have probably already overused the techniques, and therefore parents come to a parenting class to learn more effective, long-lasting, and more humane ways to teach their children appropriate behavior.

So how can you stop the biting? Stay close so you can catch your child in the process of biting. Give a blood-curdling scream, pick up your child, and say *no!* Take the child to his room and shut the door for a couple minutes. Once a bite happens, and the other child cries, the biter is already rewarded and your lesson will not be as effective.

Avoid frustrating situations in which biting is likely to occur. Make your child take care of the bitten person by putting on disinfectant. Tell the child again and again, "You may not bite people. Use words, not teeth." You might hand the child a pillow and say, "Bite this pillow instead." As language skills increase, biting tends to decrease.

Hyperactivity

Question: My child has been diagnosed with attention deficit hyperactivity disorder (ADHD). He has difficulty making decisions, is absent-minded, and has trouble listening and following through with requests—and when he wants something, he wants it right now. I'm glad I know it's a disorder he was born with and it's not just my ineffectiveness as a parent that's causing this, but I still need help disciplining him. I'm not sure I can survive!

Answer: To keep your hyperactive child from becoming a headache, you'll need to apply these seven disciplinary rules:

1. Be firm and establish clear ground rules.

2. Make a choice for your child rather than flooding him with petty time-consuming decisions. If he dawdles and shows indecisiveness over such things as what to wear or what to clean up first, you decide. Your decisiveness will keep your child from arguing about insignificant things.

3. Establish one or two routine chores your child must do. It's a mistake not to require any chores because it's too much trouble to see that he does what is asked.

4. Be prepared for your child's absentmindedness. Active children need reminders, but avoid getting irritated and saying, "I've told you a million times." Patiently keep on your child's case until the job is done. Short lists help. They're impersonal, and your child will gain satisfaction as he checks off tasks completed.

5. Be sure your child hears you and understands what you have said. Get his attention, look in his eyes, and make your request in slow, deliberate language. Then have him repeat the request to make sure he understands.

6. If your child tends to be disorganized in his thinking and behavior, you may have to calmly ask "who, what, where, and when" questions to get the necessary information.

7. Teach your child manners. He can learn to wait his turn and not interrupt. Use your common sense. If you're on the phone and you can say to the person you're talking to, "Just a minute, my son needs to tell me something," don't frustrate him by trying to make him wait. But if you feel his behavior is abnormally disruptive, you must correct firmly. Don't let your child be unduly loud and noisy in public. Do something quickly to stop out-of-bounds behavior, even if it's momentarily embarrassing. Saying "Wait till we get home" isn't going to help this type of child!

Once you begin to use these rules and find other methods that work, you may have to occasionally run interference for your overactive child. Don't downgrade him in front of others, or make excuses so he feels he can get away with something. But if teachers, Scout leaders, or parents of his friends are struggling to find ways to curb his unruly behavior and get him to pay attention, share what you've learned.

And now a word of hope. Although you can't expect some magical cure, or that your child will be different as a teenager, he will, with your patient teaching, learn effective ways to cope with his activity level, so he won't be as disruptive. The most important thing you must remember is that your child, despite his disabilities, needs your acceptance in order to feel personal value.

Whining

Question: I've got a whiner. I thought by 7 years of age she would have outgrown this childish behavior, but she hasn't. There's nothing I dislike more than grown-ups who sulk and whine when things don't go their way. What can I do to stop the whining?

Answer: Take a survey among your friends who have children between the age of 2 and 8. How many of them have children who whine? Chances are 99.6 percent do. Whining is a typical childish behavior.

Now, consider when your child whines. Is this scene familiar? You're cooking dinner, the stew just boiled over, the sink is clogged, guests are due in five minutes, and your 3-year-old is whining, "Mommy, Mommy," for no particular reason.

Or has this ever happened? You've spent the day dragging your reluctant 4- and 7-year-olds around to every department store within a 60-mile radius, ripping off their clothes, trying on new ones, and parading them in front of the mirror. All the time the children are whining, "I want to go home." At the end of the day, with enough clothing to cover 10 suntanned, naked bodies, you announce, "It's time to go home." Then, of course, junior whines, "I don't want to go home," looks around, and spots a stuffed dinosaur that's twice as long as he is, and announces, "I want that." You ignore his plea. It doesn't go away. He says all the important things such as "please," "forgive me," "I'm sorry," and "you're welcome," in an effort to hit your yes button, but nothing works. So all the way home he whines, "You never buy me anything."

Or maybe you can relate to this one: You finally say yes to your boss's invitation for dinner. "Bring the kids," you've been told. And you make the fatal mistake—you do. Dinner at 7:00 turns out to be served at 8:00, and by the time the entrée is placed in front of your children's sleepy heads they force open an eye and begin to whine, "I hate that." The host brings them peanut butter sandwiches. More whining: "I want jelly on it." And when jelly is added, they whine, "I'm not hungry."

Why do children whine? It's a childish, immature method to get a message across for those who don't seem to understand words and more subtle attention-getting behavior.

How do you get rid of the whining? The child's own growing-up process will help. But whining can become a habit that's hard to break. So let's go back to the three scenarios and figure out the reason for the whining, and what to do about it.

Scene 1: You're too busy to pay any attention to your child—so she whines. Give her attention after the whining, and you'll reward her and end up with more whining. The answer is to give attention at the first sign of attention-getting behavior, and if the whining continues, ignore it. A time-out may help. It's not much fun to whine in the privacy of your own room.

Scene 2: The child is tired, and everything the host tries to do to please ends up with more whining. The answer is to meet the child's needs, not his wants. He wanted peanut butter and jelly, but he needed to be put to bed!

Scene 3: Children whine when they want something they can't have. If you never give children anything they whine for, the whining shouldn't last more than a year or two.

Premature sexual behavior

Question: Recently I caught my two sons (ages 4 and 6) with two neighborhood girls (ages 6 and 8), all with their pants down. The 8-year-old girl was instructing the younger girl to press her pelvic area up to my son, who was leaning against a tree. Then she said the boys should put their "penis in here," pointing to the correct spot.

My husband and I talked to the girls' parents, who say they have never had a "bad" movie in their house nor any magazines to show such things, but that the girls had watched their dogs mate.

We talked to the children and agreed to "discipline" them by keeping them indoors for a week and not allowing them to play together outside of our yards. But I still don't trust those girls! Do you think this girl had seen the sexual act from a magazine, a movie, or was told by someone, or does this kind of sexual interest come naturally at that age? Should we allow them to continue to play together? Do children under the age of puberty feel any sexual sensations? What should I say to my boys when I notice an erection caused by touching themselves?

Answer: Children this age are interested in their bodies and will explore their genitals and discover the pleasant sensation of touch. For boys, this can lead to an erection. And yes, children do experience sexual feelings before puberty. When this happens, simply explain, "God made your genitals to be very sensitive to touch. They are private and special and not to be played with. That's why we keep them covered and don't touch them except to keep them clean." When curiosity is satisfied, children usually go on to other things.

Curiosity can lead to sexual experimentation among children. It might very well be that after watching dogs mate, a child might ask if people do it the same way. This might lead to the answer "Yes, a daddy puts his penis into a mommy's vagina, and that's the way they have a baby." Add to this a few bedroom scenes from the soap operas, and you can see how children might role-play "having a baby." It's important to give your children correct information, but if you see them using this information in sexual play, you must explain that any play using their private or sexual body parts is not appropriate. This is something special for mommies and daddies.

If sexual play continues, or you notice that the children are becoming secretive in their play and look guilty when you come close, you may want to carefully supervise and limit their time together. Establish the policy "no closed doors," and make sure when your children play at the neighbors' house that the same policies apply and that supervision is available.

Once children experience sexual stimulation prematurely, through self-manipulation to climax, sexual experimentation with peers, or adult abuse, it is almost impossible for them to go back to what we call "childhood innocence." Without thinking, these children may act in ways that they have found create feelings of sexual pleasure, by masturbating or rubbing back and forth when sitting on a person's lap, only to be rejected and shamed because of the inappropriateness of their behavior. The result is increased guilt and often an even greater desire for more sexual stimulation. It's a hard cycle to break, and a child may need professional help.

It's not easy to give your children the sexual information needed to satisfy curiosity without creating sexual hang-ups in the future, and yet guard them from sexual experimentation that may lead to premature sexual responses. A trip to the library may help you find just the resource you're looking for.

Tattling

Question: How can I teach my children to solve their own problems? Right now I have two tattletales. If either one of them does something or says something the other thinks might be worthy of punishment, I get a full report. I've tried ignoring, but this doesn't seem to work. Is this a natural part of sibling rivalry, or do my children have overly sensitive consciences?

Answer: My guess is that the tattletale problem you have with your children may be some sibling rivalry mixed in with active consciences. But your reaction to their tattling will either encourage or discourage it.

Children learn to tattle on each other when there is something in it for them. You may think you are ignoring the tattling, but even the look of shock on your face can be enough of a reward to cause the tattling to continue.

The question is Do you want to cut yourself off from all "intelligence" reports? If you do, in addition to ignoring the reports, send the tattler to his room for five minutes' time-out each time the tattling occurs. If you don't, you must begin patiently teaching your child what should be reported and what should not.

How can a child distinguish between something that needs to be reported to you for parental interference and what should be ignored? The three basic household rules may be a beginning: 1. You may not hurt yourself. 2. You may not hurt others. 3. You may not hurt things.

When the child comes to you with a bit of trivia that doesn't need your intervention, you can respond in a number of ways:

First, you can put a sense of responsibility for stopping this misconduct on the shoulders of the tattler. "What did you do to stop what's happening?" "What do you think you should do?" "Don't you think you'd better go back and try to solve the problem?" If you offer to help solve the problem, your involvement will reward the tattler. You might also express how you feel about tattling: "I feel irritated when you run to me tattling on each other when you are capable of solving the problem!"

Second, you can affirm the child for noninvolvement. "It's a good thing you left the scene of the crime, so you wouldn't get hurt or suffer any consequences for this. Perhaps you should go to your room for a while until things are settled." This approach is especially beneficial when you need to stop the activity that's been reported. By removing the tattler from the administration of consequences, the reward for tattling is less. Plus, if the offending child doesn't know your source of information, there is less chance for resentment toward the sibling.

Third, you can presume that both are guilty. (This is often the case with tattling.) One eggs the other on and then chickens out and tells on the most gullible! If you suspect this, say, "There needs to be a consequence to teach you that this is unacceptable behavior. What consequence do you think would teach both of you this lesson?" After a number of ideas have been presented, a choice of the most effective consequence will need to be made. If they can't decide, say, "I will make the decision, and neither of you will like it."

Cleaning rooms

Question: Why don't children like to clean their rooms? All of my friends seem to be having the same problem with their children as I have with my daughter.

Answer: Let's turn that question around. Think of some things your children really like to do and ask them what makes these things so appealing.

Probably it's fun. Friends are doing it. Their friends value this activity. They want to impress their friends. Others appreciate what they're doing. Others notice. It enhances a skill that is important to them. It's a challenge for them to beat their own performance or the performance of others. It helps them toward a goal they want to accomplish. It diverts their minds from problems or things they don't like to do. They get rewards that are meaningful to them. It's easy and doesn't seem like work. It makes them happy. It makes others happy. It makes them feel competent. They take personal ownership and have an investment in the outcome. And the list could go on.

Now, to solve the problem of children not liking to clean their rooms, all you have to do is build the above elements into the task and you should end up with children who love to clean their rooms! Impossible?

For most of us, the challenge is too great. There are too many factors to turn around, and it's just easier to nag, threaten, and demand. This, however, is counterproductive and makes children resist even more.

Those children who do seem to enjoy keeping their rooms orderly (and yes, there are a few in this world) seem to have an inborn need for orderliness. Sometimes these children become perfectionists, wanting everything in their environment to be perfect. And this trait, although it may serve to keep rooms neat, can become a burden on the children whose expectations exceed their capability to control their world. Their drive for perfection causes them to push themselves and others. Often these children grow up to be very difficult people to live with.

Somewhere there has to be a happy medium. If your children don't seem to have a neat bone in their bodies, you're going to have to provide some crutches.

Think about how you can make the task fun, easy, challenging, rewarding, something that others notice or makes others happy, and is internally satisfying.

Perhaps the problem lies somewhat in the idea of ownership. If it's the "children's room," why can't they determine how it's kept? Why do their parents' standards of cleanliness have to apply to their domain? Maybe parents should give their children only their bed and a corner of the closet, and reserve for themselves ownership of the floor and furniture, along with the right to determine whether or not things belonging to the children can be left on them for more than 24 hours without a rental fee! What do you think?

Chapter 19

The Challenging Years With Older Children

What good parenting gives our children is a running start in life, not lifelong immunity from difficulties.—Elizabeth Hormann.

School-age children and teens have their own sets of problems. Here are 13 typical questions that parents have asked, with an answer based on easy obedience principles.

- Attention deficit disorder
- Disruptive behavior
- Dawdling
- Self-motivation
- Correction versus criticism
- Irresponsibility
- Disrespect
- Homework
- Chores
- More on chores
- Allowance
- Money
- Dishonesty
- Control

Attention deficit disorder (ADD)

Question: My son is 7 and has just been diagnosed as having the ADD syndrome. He has tested as being at the fifth-grade level, even though he is not doing very well in school. His teacher is understanding about his talking to his friends when he should be working independently, not listening to instructions, daydreaming, and jumping out of his seat. This was not the case last year! I now have a label for his behavior (ADD), but I really don't know what I can do about it.

Answer: The attention deficit disorder is a catchall syndrome that is tagged on children who have difficulty paying attention to things that hold little meaning for them. Other than in this area, ADD behavior differs widely among children. ADD is not a disease but a condition. It's something that has to be lived with, understood, and gently molded. Looking at this syndrome positively will help you cope. I have sometimes wished ADD stood for active developing discoverer, because in positive terms that's what your son is, an active developing discoverer who needs to use all his senses and body movement to learn. His intense curiosity drives him to jump from one thing to another, leaving a wake of unfinished projects. At 7 his body and mind are rapidly developing—and he needs you and his teachers to be understanding. He may always be more active, inattentive, forgetful, and talkative, but if he feels good about himself, he can learn ways to compensate so he doesn't disrupt the society (home and school) in which he lives! Just don't expect over- night miracles!

Your child is bright. Most ADD children are. That's one reason mundane activities and instructions at school don't hold their attention. They need challenges that stimulate their minds and at the same time keep their bodies active. When you find this magic combination, you'll notice that your son's ADD symptoms will tend to disappear. But realistically, it's hard to find this in a typical school situation, in which a teacher is responsible for 25 or 30 children!

Here are some things I'd suggest to help increase your son's attention:

1. Get his attention before you give him an instruction. (Don't interrupt him when he is absorbed in another task.)

2. Have him use as many of his senses as possible to prove to you that he has heard and understands the instruction. (Tell it, write it down, act it out as he is repeating your instruction, go to where the task is to be done, etc.)

3. Go to where the task is to be done before giving instructions—and then give only one instruction at a time, keeping on his case until it is finished. (Don't get angry and frustrated at his seeming irresponsibility—that will only make him feel bad about himself and lessen his respect for you as an authority figure.)

4. Make a game out of the task, to increase his motivation.

5. Reward immediately for small pieces of the task accomplished. These children thrive on immediate gratification.

6. Leave only a few things out in his room. Too many things become distracting, and at the end of the day his room will be a colossal mess that is too big for him to handle without great protest and tears.

7. Pray for understanding teachers, Scout and church school leaders, neighbors, and friends. If you can keep him feeling good about himself and willing to learn compensation skills, he should make a wonderful, understanding active teacher or Scout leader someday!

Disruptive behavior

Question: We have four children, ranging from 8 years to 9 months. They get along fine when our oldest is gone, but when Jason is around, everyone falls apart. There is so much conflict that it makes me miserable. His behavior is destroying our family.

Although Jason isn't hyperactive, he has trouble paying attention and getting his schoolwork done (even though he falls in the gifted range) unless he takes Ritalin, which has been prescribed only for school these past three years. It makes a significant difference in his behavior. When he doesn't take it, he makes up excuses such as "I forgot my pill, so I can't be good."

At home Jason is extremely negative. He always thinks everyone is out to get him. If one of the other kids puts a toy in the wrong place, he throws a fit and cries. He argues over everything, especially when I ask him to do anything. We've tried praise, paying him, spanking him, and telling him he has to earn money to buy his own toys, but nothing works. My other children enjoy helping out, and I'm wondering what kind of influence he is having on them. I sure hope you can help us. A big thing we need to work on is his self-esteem, but we don't know how.

Answer: You are right. Jason needs a big dose of self-esteem, but unfortunately it doesn't come in a prescription bottle. I have a feeling that Jason has an eight-year history of being a difficult child, so don't expect an overnight miracle.

Here is what has probably happened. Jason was a demanding baby, and you reacted at times with frustration and anger, causing him to react with negative behavior, which in turn ruffled your feathers, and now a pattern of interaction has been set up that is hard to break.

Here's what I suggest: Make sure he's on a good diet that's high in fruits and vegetables and low in sugar, animal products, and processed foods. Many times, allergies cause behavior problems. Consult with your pediatrician about the effect of Ritalin not being given during the hours he is home. Would it be worth trying a steady dose throughout the day, to see if this might improve his home behavior enough so you could start reacting more positively to him? Although drugs should not be considered a cure-all, this might break your negative cycle of interactions. And it would take away his handy excuse for not behaving: "I forgot to take my pill." He must begin taking responsibility for his behavior.

At the same time, you need to learn how to react to Jason in such a way that he doesn't become defensive and defiant. A good ongoing parenting class taught by a professional counselor is what I suggest. You need to be given ideas one week, go try them, and come back for an evaluation and more ideas. If you can't find a parenting class, then I'd strongly suggest family counseling. The earlier you can be retrained in how to interact with Jason in a positive way, the earlier you'll begin to see improvements in Jason's behavior.

Dawdling

Question: I've got a 9-year-old who is as slow as molasses. It takes him hours to do something that should take only a few minutes. I tell him to brush his teeth, and 30 minutes later it's still not done. What can I do to hurry him along?

Answer: Here are four possible answers to the molasses problem:

1. A child's concept of time is not the same as an adult's. An hour to you might seem like only a few minutes to a child, and vice versa. If this is the problem, maturity will help—and you're just going to have to be patient.

2. Even adults differ when it comes to speed. You and your child may be programmed differently, and you'll have to accept this difference.

3. There may be too many distractions between your request and the place where it must be carried out. Put a TV set between the breakfast table and the bathroom sink, and it may take 30 minutes to get those teeth brushed!

4. Finally, a child may be purposely moving at a snail's pace to "win" or get back at you. We call this passive-aggressive behavior. The child won't kick and scream, he'll merely rebel by doing nothing! In this case you've got to defuse your child's hidden anger with some active listening and start building a little rapport. Good luck!

Self-motivation

Question: My oldest son just turned 10. He has many beautiful qualities, but he isn't self-motivated. He is smart, but misses school assignments, which brings his grade down. When I tell him to go to his room to study, he goes, but he gets distracted with other things. He is overweight, loses his cool quickly, and is impulsive. How can I help him become self-motivated?

Answer: If only I knew the magic formula for self-motivation, I could make a fortune. There are millions of parents out there who would give anything for the answer—and a good majority of them have boys just about your son's age!

Your child needs to feel good about himself. Where does he shine? What are his interests? Many times finding success in one area spills over into other areas.

Second, if your child has a distraction problem and you want the homework done or the multiplication tables learned, you've got to be willing to sit with him and feed him immediate rewards for his efforts. Celebrate when the first problem is done. Getting an A on a paper is not an immediate enough reward for unmotivated children.

And third, it would surely help if your son could find a challenging school environment, probably one in which a child can advance at his own rate, in which immediate rewards (not grades) are built into the program, and in which he won't be compared to others. The complaint of many unmotivated children is "There's always someone better; why should I try?" But finding this type of an educational program is difficult, and finding it at a cost you can afford may be almost impossible.

In most large cities there are *expensive* reading or math tutorial programs. But I've discovered that they are usually only as effective as the instructors. A wide variety of methods work *if* the teacher in the process communicates these messages: "You are special. I like you. You have so many talents. This work is easy-breezy—you can do it. You're one super-bright kid. You can do anything you want to do." Get the idea?

I sometimes think hiring an older teenager to come over to play basketball or draw pictures (or whatever) with your child for an hour while pumping him full of this type of positive talk can be just as effective as expensive tutorial programs. Why not give it a try?

The bottom line is, your child won't be self-motivated until he has a good reason to be self-motivated. And right now your son is probably operating on one or both of the following premises: either it's more effort than it's worth, or why try and chance failure? If you can find a way to change his negative self-talk, then you will have found the secret to self-motivation.

Correction versus criticism

Question: My children need correction at times, and yet I know that criticism kills a child's sense of value. How can I help them become better people and learn what they need to learn without becoming a nagging, critical person?

Answer: Follow these three guidelines:

Guideline 1: Correct with honey, not a hammer. In other words, make your correction as sweet as possible. Say what you have to say firmly, but with a smile, a lilt in your voice, and a gentle touch. Let the effect of your words and your body language say "I care about you. That's why I'm telling you this."

If you question the effectiveness of this method, put it to the test. First, try the hammer approach, hitting your child with the full impact of your correction. Raise your voice, make your words sharp and staccato, glare at the offender, and take a rigid stance. You'll get your kids' attention, and they'll probably do what you ask, but they'll resent your criticism.

Second, try the same words but this time use a little honey—make your words and actions sweet—and see if it doesn't stick without causing ego damage.

Guideline 2: Sandwich your correction between words of appreciation. Start your correction with something positive: "I appreciate your helping me set the table; just remember next time to put the knife on the right side and the fork on the left." And then you might want to add, "And by the way, the centerpiece looks great."

Guideline 3: Correct in private—and keep it that way. When you correct your child, do it in such a way that you don't broadcast his mistake to the world. After Kevin had done something wrong, I remember him pleading, "Don't tell Daddy." But as soon as his dad walked into the house, Kevin told him all about what he had done. He just didn't want someone else doing it.

Irresponsibility

Question: The only way I can get my 8- and 11-year-olds to get up, get dressed, and eat their breakfast so they won't be late for school is to scream and threaten. I hate myself for being this way, but nothing else seems to work.

Answer: Children respond to screams and threats because they know if they don't, they will get it! Your children now need to be retrained.

There are two major ways of changing a child's behavior. The first is to reward the behavior you want. Behavior that is positively reinforced is usually repeated. This method is by far the most pleasant and pain-free way to change a child's behavior. But it doesn't always bring the immediate results that you want, so parents resort to the second method, in which a consequence is imposed.

But for best results, I'd suggest a combination of the two, offering both a reward for responsibility and a consequence for irresponsibility.

Now, let's apply these methods to your situation. First, the reward. How much do you think the job of getting your kids up and off to school is worth? Would you pay someone a dollar? Why not make the following proposal to your kids: "Kids, how would you like to earn a dollar every morning for the job of bossing someone around? Frankly, I'm tired of bossing you around, making sure you get up and dressed and get your breakfast eaten, and I'm ready to hire someone else to do it. You can have the job if you want it. The job starts at 7:00 a.m. and ends at 8:00 a.m., when you're in the car, ready to be taken to school."

Next, the consequence. "If you miss the 8:00 a.m. deadline, you will lose a quarter for every minute the person you are bossing around is late getting into the car."

If your children take you up on the job offer, reward them immediately. Let them feel the dollar bill in their hands as they tumble into the car at 7:59. But if it's 8:01, too bad! They get only 75 cents. And if it's 8:05, they owe you a quarter!

I think you'll be surprised how well a method like this works. For some children who are easily distracted, you may need to make the reward more frequent—a quarter if they get dressed by 7:15, another one if they are at the breakfast table by 7:30, another if they finish eating by 7:45, and the final one if they get their teeth brushed, gather their books, and are in the car by 8:00.

The only way a program like this will work is if you are consistent. Don't be soft and give them a dollar if the clock says 8:02. They have to know you mean what you say.

If you think this method sounds expensive, remember that the wage earners (your children) can now have the responsibility of using their money to buy their own clothing and school supplies. Who knows, this method may actually be less expensive for you than handing out money every time your child wants something.

Plus, you don't have to keep paying them forever. Once the habit is established, there is no longer a need for this reward system. The freedom of self-discipline becomes a reward in itself.

Disrespect

Question: How do I stop my 12-year-old from treating me disrespectfully? He says things such as "I don't have to listen to you," or "You don't know anything," or "You're a _________." My husband sometimes says these things when he's angry, but I don't think it's right for a child to talk to his mother like that.

Answer: It's not only wrong for a child to talk disrespectfully to his mother, but also wrong for a husband to talk that way to a wife. The longer you allow this practice to continue, the harder it will be to stop. You must nip this disrespectful behavior in the bud and preserve your own dignity and personhood. In doing this, you may be saving a future wife and children from being hurt with words and actions that will destroy them psychologically or lead to physical battering.

Unfortunately, children today are bombarded with sitcoms and movies in which crude, ugly, demeaning things are said. Have you ever seen the person who uses this filthy, disrespectful language punished, or called to account for it? It's easy to see how children hear this stuff and begin to think it's the way to talk. They experiment with foul language with their peers and in school. And do the teachers stop them? No! That would be against the freedom of speech—the freedom to destroy others with words.

We need to forbid our children to use disrespectful language in our homes. The role of language in shaping behavior has been well documented in research journals. Our decision-making process is shaped by words in our minds. Impressions become stronger when words are spoken. And actions often follow. Abusive words can lead to abusive behavior.

First, you must get the cooperation of your husband. I'm sure he doesn't want his son to grow up thinking it's OK to treat women disrespectfully, and yet—"like father, like son." If your husband has any fatherly guts at all, he will apologize to you and then to his son, saying, "I have sometimes said things to your mother that I shouldn't have. I was wrong to have done this, and I will not let a son of mine treat his mother disrespectfully. If in anger I forget and do it again, please stop me. We men have to stick together and protect the women in our family. We must never tear them down. Do you understand?"

Second, determine with your children what consequence there should be if anyone in the family treats another disrespectfully. It might be anything from apologizing and saying three kind things about the person, to giving the person the right to use the "abuser" as a servant for 24 hours, or it might mean losing a privilege.

Third, assert your parental right to be a benevolent dictator and turn off any music, TV program, or movie in which disrespectful words are being used. Make a stand and say, "I will not have that kind of language heard in my home. Period!"

Homework

Question: I hate homework! I'm 35 years old and shouldn't have to worry about homework. But if I don't, my kids would never get theirs done. What can I do to get my 8- and 10-year-olds to do their own homework?

Answer: Are you convinced that homework is good for your kids? If you're not, you're going to have a hard time convincing them! Here's what the experts (those who hand out the assignments) say about homework. It helps students remember, because it reinforces what they have learned in school. It improves reading skills, raises grades, and teaches children to be responsible and self-disciplined. But good luck in trying to convince your children that homework is good for them!

Instead, set up a comfortable place where homework is to be done. Then don't let your school-age child stay there for more than 20 minutes. Too many children are made to stay long periods of time behind the closed doors of their rooms doing homework. They dawdle, they procrastinate, they read page after page without exercise or reward, accomplishing little. No wonder homework is a bore. You've got to change that!

First, forbid any homework until your children have played vigorously for one hour after school. If this means you need to get outdoors and play catch, shoot baskets, jump rope, or ride bikes with your kids, do it. You probably need the exercise too! No TV, please!

Then challenge your children to break their homework into two or three 20-minute sessions and tell you what they plan to accomplish in each session. Help them be realistic. Make sure they understand the homework instructions and have all the materials they will need so they can concentrate for the full time. Give them the choice of one of three possible rewards if they beat the clock. Let them set the buzzer and push themselves to accomplish what they set out to do. As soon as the 20 minutes are over, get them out of their room, finished or not. Then 40 minutes of play before another 20-minute session. Try to get in two study sessions before supper.

Give them a worthwhile incentive if they can accomplish all of their homework in two sessions, so they don't have to come back for an after-supper session. Forty minutes of daily homework is plenty for school-age children.

What kind of rewards would be appropriate after each session? What about calling a friend, 15 minutes of parent time doing whatever the child wishes, Mom doing one of the child's chores (be sure to be specific), 15 minutes of television time, or money, especially if the child has his or her own account for personal needs and savings?

Check the quality of the work before handing out the reward, but don't be a perfectionist. You want your children to enjoy the learning process.

Doing homework to keep them from flunking or to get a good grade does not generally motivate children this age. If they do their homework in the allotted amount of time, their should be an immediate reward. If they don't meet their goal because they ran into a problem, reward them for effort so that they don't get frustrated. But if they failed because they dawdled, too bad!

Once children get trained into a routine, homework won't be such a pain.

Chores

Question: How do you get kids to do their chores without complaining? My boys make me feel like I'm a slave driver every time I ask them to do something!

Answer: Think about it. What makes a slave a slave? No choice. Threat of punishment. No reward for a task well done. No sense of ownership or personal benefit. No feeling of significance. The jobs are routine and menial, and the work is never done—like "Ol' Man River," it just keeps rollin' along. If your children feel like you're using them to do all the unpleasant tasks around the house merely because they are free labor, no wonder they feel like slaves!

The slave problem has little to do with the tasks themselves; it's an attitude problem. You've got to change your own thinking, and eventually your children's, into seeing tasks that need to be done not as chores but as contributions.

We all love to make contributions to various projects. Whether we give money, skills, or time, we feel our contribution has made a difference. The internal sense of personal value is enhanced, and many times we need no other reward. We will stop helping the minute we feel what we're doing is becoming a chore. Chores are what you do when you have no choice!

Relating this concept to your children and household tasks, you've got to figure out how to help them feel that everything they do at home is a contribution to the family's welfare and in some way will benefit them, either with personal satisfaction or material gain.

Keeping the slave model in mind, you're going to have to turn chores into contributions. Here are some ideas:

1. Give your children a choice.
2. Change tasks on a daily, weekly, or monthly basis so the tasks don't get boring.
3. Allow your children to tackle tasks that challenge them, so they have more of an opportunity for personal growth and satisfaction.
4. Be quick to notice something good, and mention it specifically. "The sink sparkles. And I really appreciate your cleaning the bathroom without my having to remind you. Thanks." Be generous with words of appreciation.
5. Be miserly when it comes to criticism. Pad it by first noticing something positive. Then instruct rather than criticize. Then add more padding with another compliment. "The sink sparkles. You may want to use some cleaner around the base of the faucet to get off the mineral deposits caused by standing water. What would this family do without your good help? Thanks."
6. Help your children to see that they are making a valuable contribution to the family's welfare. Make them feel significant. Give them incentives. Be quick to reward a job well done. And in return, give *them* a hand when needed.

More on chores

Question: My 12-year-old refuses to do any chores. She seems to think that because we brought her into the world we should provide her with expense-free living, without her having to lift a finger. How can I make her understand that she needs to do her fair share?

Answer: You must make sure your daughter knows without a shadow of a doubt that with privilege there is responsibility. The privilege of belonging to your family carries the responsibility of sharing the work your family generates, whether it's trash removal, food preparation, washing laundry, or house and yard maintenance.

Children should not have to be paid for basic "home" work. But if they carry their fair share of these responsibilities, then they should enjoy the privileges of a fair share of the income to use to meet their personal needs, through an allowance. But no "home" work, no privileges! During the training time you must be strong and not rescue her when she desperately needs money. But once she is cooperating with the family policies by doing her fair share, then you're free to give an occasional gift or bonus to reward her for working above and beyond the call of duty.

Doing useful labor around the home is an essential part of a child's character development. It teaches children to be responsible, it helps them develop worthwhile skills and abilities, and it reinforces the truism that nothing worthwhile comes free. Having a house, a car, pets, or a yard takes work. Having a fresh strawberry pie for supper takes work. Either you work so it can be purchased, or you make it yourself.

What you are experiencing with your daughter is common with children this age. Some parents feel the hassle it takes to squeeze a little help out of a child isn't worth it! *But it is.* You just have to learn techniques of making "home" work attractive, meaningful, and fun. It may help you to follow these suggestions:

First, *never call a task a chore.* The word "chore" sounds dreadful and scares away most children. Plus, it gives the idea that home responsibilities are a drudgery and something to be avoided. Rather, call it a job, a task, a privilege, a joy, an honor. Anything but a chore.

Second, *make the job a challenge.* Every 3-year-old I know loves to do the dishes—but very few 13-year-olds do. I'm convinced that the difference is not the age so much as the challenge of the task. At 3 doing the dishes is a fantastic challenge. At 13 it's a bore. The challenge at age 13 is shopping for the ingredients or cooking the dinner. Vary tasks. Give her a choice. Trade tasks with your daughter. Work along with her. Praise her for a job well done. Turn chores into challenges and make sure she realizes that privilege requires responsibility.

Allowance

Question: I'm trying to decide whether I should give my school-age children an allowance. They have everything they need, and if it's reasonable, I'll get them what they want. But since the neighbor kids get an allowance, they think they should get one too.

Answer: Children love money. Money means freedom to get what one wants without having to depend upon parents. With money, children can buy pleasure, power, and prestige. And they will, if you give them money with no built-in accountability. Allowance should be given on two conditions: first, the child does something to "earn" it (even if it's just setting the table and brushing his or her teeth); and second, once earned it is spent responsibly.

Some say you should give kids an allowance because you love them, not because of what they earn or how they spend it. But I don't believe in mixing love and money. Children should be loved because they exist. But just because they exist doesn't mean they should be given money! To do so without built-in accountability courts irresponsibility. Plus, you're setting yourself up for future accusations of "If you really loved me, you'd increase my allowance." It also promotes jealousy when one child receives more money than another. For example, if Grandma gives more to one grandchild than another, it gives the message that Grandma loves that child more. In reality, Grandma loves both the same and wisely makes her decision to give one child more than another because one has a greater need.

An allowance without accompanying responsibility or as a message of love may be more harmful than helpful. So before buckling under to the pressure of "But Jason's folks give him an allowance," think clearly about what you want your child to learn from an allowance—and whether an allowance is the best way to teach that lesson.

In general, don't give an allowance unless you . . .

1. *Decide how the money is to be used.* If there is no plan for savings, giving to church or other charitable causes, or spending, then you're promoting the irresponsible use of money for pleasure, power, and prestige.

2. *Determine how much money the child needs.* Work out a yearly or monthly budget with your child. What are the child's monetary needs? How much is needed for clothing, entertainment, toys, and food (such as candy bars, gum, and soda, that aren't part of the family meals)? Then compute a reasonable weekly amount that the child can be responsible for. As the child gets older, a special account should be established for big needs, such as a car or college.

3. *Establish a savings account in a bank* so the money will be available when the child needs it, but won't be burning a hole in the child's pocket or be tempting him or her to break the ceramic piggy bank.

Money

Question: I'm constantly arguing with my daughter over money. She's 14 and thinks she knows better than I what she should wear and how much she should spend on entertainment or presents for her friends. She seems to have no sense of the value of money.

Answer: Stop subsidizing her. As long as you hold the purse strings, you'll never get along. Money, believe it or not, is not worth fighting over. A mother-daughter relationship is far more valuable than money. But at the same time, you don't want your daughter wasting "your" money. She's got to have her own.

I don't believe in allowances—money automatically given to children because they exist. I think there are other more positive ways to show your unconditional love than doling out money. It often fosters an irresponsible attitude. I see too many children persecuting their parents with "I don't care what you think," or "You can't make me." Then at the end of the week they pick up their allowance, thinking that their family owes it to them. Love, discipline, lessons on spiritual values, and meeting basic needs are all things parents owe their children, not money.

An allowance isn't a bad idea if it's given for a period of time for the express purpose of teaching a child how to budget money. Then the parents should be involved in making sure the child has a savings plan and is making meaningful decisions. But continuing an allowance after the basic budget lesson has been learned is not good. Instead, an allowance should be conditional on certain behavior. "It's worth it to me to give you $5 a week for your own spending money if I don't have to remind you to make your bed each morning and feed the dog each night." Then when the conditions are met and the $5 is handed over, the transaction is clean. No strings attached. The child has "earned" her money and should have the responsibility to spend it as she likes.

But if an allowance is given without conditions, parents too often get involved in how that allowance is going to be spent. Allowance (money) can become a powerful tool that parents use to get their children to do what they want. "If you don't start saving some of your allowance for a rainy day, I'm going to dock your allowance." "A kid who can't get homework in on time doesn't deserve any allowance."

If your child wants to make her own financial decisions, she should have her own money. It's not unreasonable to expect a 14-year-old to earn her own spending money. There are always tasks around a house that are above and beyond the common household maintenance duties that a child can be paid to perform. Some teens do better if Mom is not their employer. Your daughter might want to establish a baby-sitting service, mow lawns, shovel walks, tutor school-age children, or bake bread and cookies for the neighbors.

Having a job for which your teen is responsible will keep your daughter too busy to get into trouble, give her a feeling of value, and provide money that she can spend without parental control. Teens want power. They want to control their own lives. How much better it is for teens to have a sense of power and control that having their own money brings than to have money be the source of continual conflict.

Dishonesty

Question: My 16-year-old daughter received my permission to stay with her girlfriend for the weekend. Instead of doing that, they both went to an empty house of one of their friends whose parents were away, and partied all weekend. When the parents returned and found out what had happened, they prosecuted. My daughter is now facing court hearings. I wasn't the only parent who was duped. Each teen had given the same excuse, and none of us checked on our children to find out what they were really doing. How can I make sure this doesn't happen again?

Answer: Your daughter has just taught you a very important lesson: you can't trust her! She's going to have to provide some substantial evidence to the contrary if you are ever to be persuaded that she's once again safe to trust. Spell out what evidence she could provide that will convince you that she has now reformed her ways and can once again be trusted.

If every day for three months she is where she says she'll be when she says she'll be there, and gives you the addresses and phone numbers so you can make sure, would that help?

She's going to resist this kind of control. "I don't want to be treated like a baby, having my mom check up on me. What will my friends think? I'd be humiliated!"

Respond with "If you won't allow me to get the evidence I need in three months so I can once again trust you with your freedom, I would be happy to wait a year. If you don't get into any trouble and are acting mature (not lying or experimenting with drugs, sex, and antisocial behavior) after one year, then I'll be willing to trust you once again and grant you the freedom you want. It's your choice: three months or a year."

Most teens, if given this choice, will go for a shorter parole and closer supervision. The goal is to teach your daughter the benefits of honesty and that freedom is the result of mature decision-making.

Make it clear that your purpose during this "parole period" is not to pry into her personal life in the hope of catching her doing something wrong, but to be available or close enough to offer her your judgment and counsel so she can check in with you for your advice before taking a chance and perhaps making a bad decision that would cause her to lose more of her freedom. Freedom is so important for teens that they will do almost anything to get it. Either they will rebel, as your daughter did when she lied about where she was spending the weekend, or they can earn it by proving to their parents they are trustworthy.

You want to make it easy for your daughter to prove to you that she has turned over a new leaf and is now trustworthy. Make it clear: either she can have freedom for responsibility, or you will impose parental supervision to control her irresponsibility.

Control

Question: We've got a very bright son who is trying to control our family. He argues with everything. Many of his arguments are quite sound, and after a time we agree with the point he is making, but it's so disruptive to our family. He seems to know his place in school and respects his teachers, but he shows no respect for us, his parents.

Answer: Beginning around 2 years of age a child's primary drive is to learn how much of the world he is responsible for controlling. That's why limits are healthy. When a child learns that there are strong people in his life who will stop him when he gets out of control and will enforce the limits, it brings the child a sense of security. He doesn't have to worry about what's beyond the boundaries. He knows someone else controls that.

A child who doesn't have the privilege of having adults in his life who are strong enough to set the limits that keep him in his place feels responsible for more than he should. This is scary to a child. Bright children, especially, are prone to feel insecure without appropriate limits. They reason, "If I'm the strongest person in my family (and I know I'm not smart enough to protect everyone), who will take care of me?" When they discover that they are "smarter" than their parents, or can outwit their parents, this is frightening. First, the child loses respect for his parents, and second, the child often attempts to control them, since the child feels he knows best!

You must establish some limits in your family, areas in which you are responsible and have control, and make this very clear to your child. If he starts to argue about something in your area of control, he needs to be stopped immediately, and you need to say, "We understand that you have strong opinions about this, but this is an area that we as parents are responsible for, and therefore, we are in control."

If the child is old enough, encourage him to write his arguments on paper, then let him know that you will carefully read his statement and call a family council to discuss his position.

Other times you can give him permission to present his case verbally. But *you* be in control and *you* give him permission. As soon as he starts to argue, say, "I can tell you have a strong opinion about this. You need to understand that Mom and Dad make the decision in this area, but we are willing to hear how the rest of the family feels. You may present your opinion now."

Healthy families allow their children to freely discuss differences in opinion. Arguing, however, which involves not being willing to respectfully listen to others who have a dissenting opinion, *is a control mechanism.* Don't allow your children to control you with this behavior.

Chapter 20

Parenting Prodigal Children

Love your children with all your heart; love them enough to discipline them before it is too late.—Lavina Christensen Fugal, on being chosen Mother of the Year, 1955.

Thousands of conscientious Christian parents suffer excruciating pain over the prodigal behavior of their children. These kids grow up in the church, they learn all the right Bible verses, Mom and Dad have had family devotions with them every day, yet they defiantly turn their backs on their spiritual heritage and even choose to experiment with harmful habits such as smoking, drugs, alcohol, and sex.

How do you parent prodigals? Do you kick them out—or welcome them home? The answer isn't clear-cut, but the goals of easy obedience still stand. Ask yourself these questions:

1. Will what I do help my children to become self-disciplined?
2. Will what I do avoid or resolve conflict?
3. Will what I do preserve or build my children's feelings of self-worth?

A good model to follow is the father in Jesus' parable of the prodigal son (Luke 15:11-32).

- The father didn't try to force his wayward son to stay home.
- The father gave him what was rightfully his.
- The father didn't keep helping him once the initial support was squandered. He let his son hit bottom.
- The father waited and watched, but he didn't let his son's behavior destroy his own life. He didn't blame himself.
- The father ran toward his repentant son, welcoming him with open arms and full reinstatement into the family.
- The father didn't lecture or say "I told you so."
- The father celebrated.

Prodigal children need a strong dose of unconditional love combined with limits. Regardless of age, children must feel accepted. But if they choose to hurt others with their rebelliousness, then there must be consequences. In love, you cannot allow your children to mistreat anyone—including yourself.

The prescription of unconditional love and limits, sometimes termed "tough love," is easy enough to verbalize—but the difficulty comes in the application.

Limits

Rhonda was a prodigal living at home. Heavy metal, cultism, alcohol, and pot were a common part of her lifestyle, and it clashed head-on with the values of the rest of the family.

With three younger and very impressionable children, Mom felt she must take a stand. As much as she loved Rhonda, she could not allow her to flaunt her deviant lifestyle and destroy one or all of her vulnerable siblings. So with tough love Mom laid down the law. Her daughter could not disturb the rest of the family. She gave Rhonda three rules for conduct in the house:

1. No signs of drinking or smoking in any part of the house outside her room. For example, no beer cans in the refrigerator or ashtrays by the TV, and no smoke odor in the rest of the house.
2. You can listen to whatever music you want to in the privacy of your own room, as long as it can't be heard outside your room.
3. You may not entertain friends in your room with alcohol, smoking, cultish activities, or heavy metal.

Rhonda's mother told her that as long as she was willing to abide by the established family policies, she would be welcome to stay. But if she chose not to abide by them, she must leave. Rhonda's mother said, "I pray that you will not have to leave, but if you do I will help you find an apartment, pay two months' rent to help you get established, and then you'll be on your own. If things get tough, I want you to know I will not help support the lifestyle you have chosen.

"If you want to come back home, you'll always be welcome, but the same conditions apply. If you break them the second time, it will be entirely up to you to establish yourself elsewhere. Only once will I pay the rent to help you get established.

"I believe I am doing this for your own good. I love you and always will, but I cannot allow you to destroy the lives of those around you. I pray that someday in the future you will understand."

That next week Rhonda defiantly threw a pot party in her room. Mom calmly walked in and asked the kids to leave. When they hesitated she told them the consequences. Since pot was illegal, she would have to call the police. That was the end of the party—and the next week Rhonda was in her own apartment.

I can't report that Rhonda immediately repented with a complete change of lifestyle. Like most prodigals, including the biblical one, it took a while. But not shielding Rhonda from the consequences of her behavior was an important step in the recovery process.

In sharing this story, I am not suggesting that other families should have the same rules. Some parents may set the limits of no smoking, alcohol or other drugs, or heavy metal rock in the home, and clearly spell out the consequences for disobedience. The important thing is that limits are set and enforced. The earlier you establish those limits, the better. Waiting until your child is experimenting with these things before making the rules will cause your child more resentment than if he or she has grown up knowing this was family policy.

Dealing with blame and guilt

One of the means that rebellious children use to manipulate their parents is blame. These kids blame their folks for the mistakes the kids have made. And they keep their folks bending over backward, making excuses for their children's behavior. If your children blame you for the mistakes they make, it's time you stopped playing their game.

Bernice was overcome with guilt. Her teenage son was having a hard time, and it was all his mother's fault—at least, that's what he kept saying. When she tried to help him out, she would get "Mom, just butt out—you're always messin' things up for me." And when she left him alone to solve his own problems, she would get hit with "You don't even care about me. If you did you'd get me out of this mess!" No matter what she did, she was always wrong, and she began to feel guilty about not being able to do anything right in her son's eyes.

You've heard of child abuse? Well, I believe this constant blaming of parents for the children's own mistakes is parent abuse. Parents have to stand up for their rights; they don't have to take this abuse.

That's what Bernice did. She said, "Enough. You may not treat me like this. You make your own choices and are responsible for your own behavior—regardless of the way you were treated in childhood or what I do today. You determine your own destiny. Sure, I made some mistakes in rearing you, but I did my best. I just didn't have all the answers, and in my frustration and ignorance I mistreated you occasionally.

"But I ask you to forgive me for my mistakes. I can't go back and do it over. Saying 'I'm sorry' is the best I can do. And by doing this, I hit the ball back into your court. You can now choose whether to forgive me or keep blaming me and allow your resentment to cloud your life.

"No longer will I play your blaming game and feel guilty when you accuse me of causing your problems. In fact, I want you to know that if you continue to play this game, I will walk away, hang up, or ignore whatever you are throwing my way. I love you with all my heart, and I want what is best for you. I don't want your life eaten away by bitterness and resentment. But there's nothing I can do to prevent that if you choose to keep dwelling upon your bad memories of childhood and your perceived injustices of the present."

The result of this speech was a very surprised boy. He took the medicine in silence. Then after his mom was finished, he looked her straight in the eye and commented, "That was some speech!" But you could tell by the way he said it that even though he may not have liked it, his respect for his mom went up a notch or two.

If you at times feel your children are abusively blaming you for their mistakes, remember Bernice's speech. Stand up tall, take a deep breath, and let your children have it. Stop playing the blame game. That's the only way you'll win. And it's the only fair way to set them free to become mature individuals who are responsible for their own behavior.

Showing unconditional love

Finally, when you find yourself the parent of a prodigal child, you must be filled with unconditional love. Limits and love cannot be separated. The principle is biblical: "For whom the Lord loves he corrects" (Prov. 3:12).

When parenting your prodigal, your affection must not be dependent on your child's behavior. You must act respectfully toward him or her, even when you can't approve of what he or she is doing. This type of love has an uncanny drawing power. The story of Russ is a typical example of this:

As a young man Russ went to Vietnam and got mixed up with all kinds of things, including drugs, sex, and tobacco. His parents were obviously disappointed when he came home a chain-smoker. Russ knew how offensive smoking was to his dad, and the first time he stepped into the home with a cigarette in his hand he expected to be kicked out. Instead, his dad put an arm around him and said, "Russ, you know how I dislike smoking, but if that's the only way I can have you home, I guess I'll just have to get used to it. You're more important to me than the smoking."

Russ was so shocked with his dad's response that he never again smoked in his dad's presence. He respected his dad too much to offend him.

Of course, that is just one example—and for every positive one, there are probably a dozen negative ones. But regardless of the statistics, the winning principle remains the same: love heals alienation, while guilt and bitterness only make it fester.

So think about it. Just how accepting are you? Could you treat your prodigal with respect even if she didn't deserve it? Could you open your arms to your wayward son and lovingly introduce him to your most respected friends, or would you be ashamed to admit his existence?

Sharon and her husband hadn't heard from their son in months. David had run away, and the only thing they knew was that he was in the Los Angeles area. They asked him to write. He didn't, but that didn't keep his mom from hoping and searching. Finally, through an old friend, Sharon was able to get the address of someone who might know his whereabouts. She wrote, expressing love and a longing to see him. Would it be possible for him to meet them at the Los Angeles airport? She and Dad and Grandma and Grandpa would all be there. They were directing a tour to the Holy Land and would be taking off at 3:00 p.m.

It was just a shot in the dark. Would he get the message? And even if he did, would he make the effort to get to the airport, when he hadn't even bothered to call collect for almost a year? Sharon's faith was weak.

This was a highly esteemed Christian family. Sharon's father was a pioneer in Christian radio. His programs had aired for more than 50 years on hundreds of stations across the world. He was a giant among the Christian leadership of the country. When he led tours to the Holy Land, it was an honor to be included.

Finally the departure day came. The entire tour group was assembled in the airport boarding area. Sharon and her husband, along with Grandpa and Grandma, were surrounded by important members of the Christian community. Sharon wondered if her son had gotten the message. But it was such a remote possibility that she pushed it from her mind. With the excitement of the trip, she had almost forgotten her letter.

Just minutes before they were to board the plane, she noticed a shabby-looking couple break through the crowd. The fellow's hair and beard were unkempt and uncut. His baggy shirt (unbuttoned to the navel), cutoffs, sandals, and beads clearly identified him as part of another culture. There was so little to the girl's dress that it left no room for imagination.

Sharon's immediate thought was *How could anyone go out in public looking like that? And the nerve of them to push their way through the middle of our tour group.* She was just about to turn away when she recognized her son and immediately ran to him with arms outstretched and genuine tears of happiness. "Oh, David. You came. You came!"

Then, without any hesitation or show of embarrassment, she turned to the crowd that was watching and announced, "I would like to have you meet our son, David." There were more hugs and kisses as Dad and grandparents greeted David and welcomed his friend.

That moment was the beginning of David's homecoming. He didn't rush home, burn his clothes, and don a three-piece suit. He continued to search for himself, traveling the world and even delving into some Eastern religions. But he did begin writing, and two years later David sent his belongings home. He wasn't far behind.

Our prodigal children haven't treated us any differently from the way we have at times treated our heavenly Father. Aren't you thankful our Father is going to greet all His prodigal sons and daughters with open arms? Shouldn't we do the same?

God loves your children more than you do. He knows where they are and what they're doing. I like the picture of God being the "hound of heaven." He's not going to give up the search-and-rescue mission for your children. Although waiting is difficult, you must remember that God has ways and means of reaching the prodigals about which you have no idea. Just give Him permission to do whatever is necessary to bring them home, and while you're waiting hold on to God's promises:

"For I will contend with him who contends with you, and I will save your children" (Isa. 49:25).

"All your children shall be taught by the Lord, and great shall be the peace of your children" (Isa. 54:13).

Chapter 21

When You Don't Have an Answer—Give It to God

O bless each child of Yours,
And grant when they are grown,
They will have learned to love Your way,
And choose it for their own.

—Carol Mayes

You may try all the easy obedience techniques in this book, and still your child might have problems or exhibit some objectionable character traits. Don't be discouraged. Give God a chance to work in your child's life.

When Sara was about 6 years of age she developed an irrational fear that the house would burn down. Often at night she would complain to her mother, "I can't go to sleep. I'm afraid of a fire." Her voice would quiver, she'd cry and cling desperately to her mother, begging, "Don't leave me. I'm afraid." Her mother tried everything she could think of (talking about the fear, reasoning with her, and explaining how the smoke alarm would warn them), but nothing seemed to help.

Finally, late one night as her mom was kneeling down beside Sara's bed, talking to her about this fear, her mom said, "Sara, we haven't been able to solve this problem, so let's ask God to take away your fear." Mom put her hands on Sara's tummy and began to pray. She asked Jesus to make the spirit of fear leave Sara, to give her peace, and to help her trust in God. Sara went to sleep peacefully that night and never again experienced that intense fear.

Peter had a habit of throwing temper tantrums when he was with his father. He would scream hysterically and then hold his breath until he passed out. Peter's mother tried every new technique she learned about, but the tantrums continued. Finally she mentioned the tantrums to a Christian counselor. The counselor suggested that they first give the problem to the Lord. As they prayed together, they were impressed that

Peter was experiencing rejection. In discussing this possibility, Peter's father confessed that he had rejected Peter at the time of his birth, favoring instead his twin brother. The father repented of his negative feelings toward his son. They then prayed that God would heal the damage done to Peter's sensitive spirit. Peter never again held his breath to the point of passing out.

Jerry was accident-prone. Throughout his growing years he had broken dozens of bones and suffered numerous cuts and sprains. His mother had become fearful of having him leave her sight. She was especially concerned about his going away to college. She shared her concern with her women's Bible study group, and they began praying for her fear and for Jerry's safety.

As she prayed, she remembered that during her pregnancy she had experienced a terrible fall and was terrified that she had harmed her baby. This anxiety over Jerry's safety had continued during his growing years and seemed to increase with each accident. Once she released her irrational fear to God, she sent Jerry off to college in perfect peace. Four years later she related the story to him. "That's interesting," Jerry commented. "I haven't had an accident since I came to college."

Teresa suffered night terrors. Screaming hysterically in her sleep, she described the horrible experiences she was dreaming about, but the next morning she remembered nothing. Sometimes these terrors lasted so long that they kept Mom and Dad awake much of the night. After a long time they decided to pray for Teresa's deliverance from these irrational night terrors. They went into Teresa's bedroom shortly after she was asleep, placed their hands on Teresa's head, and asked God to do what they had not been able to do. They continued praying like this nightly as the terrors decreased in frequency. After a few weeks Teresa was sleeping calmly through the night.

Kyle had a terrible battle with his father before bedtime one night. He shouted "I hate you" to his daddy, who was so angry he slammed the door of Kyle's bedroom and threatened him if he were to get out of bed again. Kyle fell asleep with rebellion in his heart. This had happened once before, and for days afterward Kyle exhibited the spirit of rebellion.

Mom silently prayed for wisdom to know how to handle this situation without demeaning her husband and causing further conflict. She waited until both of them were asleep, then tiptoed back into Kyle's bedroom and prayed over her peacefully sleeping son. She asked that God would remove the spirit of rebellion from his heart and restore within him a loving respect for his father's authority. The next morning Kyle woke up as if nothing had happened and was once again a sweet, compliant child.

So many times parents think they are the only ones that can influence their children's thinking, and they end up forcing or "pushing the string" in the direction they want. The result is a power struggle. Whenever this happened to Elden and Esther with one of their children, they would ask the child if they could "sleep on it" for the night, and then

Elden and Esther spent much of the night in prayer, asking God that if they as parents were right in their choice, God would impress their children with the same decision. Numerous times, the next morning their children would come to them saying, "We've decided not to go," perhaps even giving a reason that the folks had not thought of, and the problem was solved without a conflict.

I'm telling you these stories to bolster your faith. God does answer prayer. The answer may not come as quickly as we feel it should. God's timetable is not the same as ours. And God's answer may not be what we expected. But when we trust Him, we can rest in the assurance that His way is best.

Working with God on behalf of our children is a cooperative effort. We have a part to do—that's why I wrote this book and why I'm so thankful you have read this far! We must be responsible disciplinarians if we want to enjoy the results of easy obedience. But we must also give our children to the Lord and ask Him to work constantly on their behalf.

If you would like to tap into God's wonderful power, I'd suggest you start by praying a blessing on your child's personality as the Bible patriarchs so often did. Ron tried praying a blessing on his children's personalities and wrote me about his experience:

> Dear Dr. Kay,
>
> I'd just like to share with you an idea that came to me while reading Genesis. I became impressed as I read over and over about the patriarchs blessing their children according to their knowledge of that child's personality and the future. Why not bless my children according to their personalities?
>
> First of all, I had to become convinced that each child's personality was a gift of God—its strengths and its weaknesses. I became aware that a child's strengths, if not properly channeled, would become weaknesses. A strength of personality turned toward oneself will destroy; turned toward God, it will bless and minister.
>
> So the direction of my blessing was to ask God to enhance the strength of my children's personalities and turn those traits toward Him. I did not want the children to change in response to Daddy's wishes; I wanted God to do the changing in them. So each night after they were asleep I would enter their room, stand over them, and pray a blessing.
>
> My oldest daughter is 10. Her most obvious personality trait is high sensitivity. She was very sensitive to herself. Her feelings were easily hurt. Tears were free-flowing. "That's not fair" was a key saying, but spoken only when she felt something was not fair to her. I prayed a blessing for her that she would be sensitive to God and others. Within two weeks change was apparent.

> Previously when disciplined, all she was concerned with was the punishment. "Am I going to get a spanking?" "How many swats?" "How long of a restriction?" Now the response is "I have done wrong; I'm sorry," and tears of genuine repentance. She has become sensitive to the feelings of others and their hurts. She is developing into a person with the ability to comfort others.
>
> I could tell of other responses in my other children, but time is too short. . . .

Ron closed the letter saying that it was his hope that other parents would pray a blessing on their children's personalities and experience God's wonderful power.

Perhaps we, as parents, try too hard to change our children's God-given personalities when we should be channeling their personalities into God's ministry. God made our children the way they are for a special calling He has for them. I believe they can be strong-willed for Jesus, hyperactive for Jesus, talkative for Jesus—or sensitive for Jesus!

But it starts with trusting in God, who gave them their personalities, that He can turn their personalities toward Himself and use them. We must pray for this; otherwise, Satan will use those same personalities to cause conflict and heartache that will ultimately destroy our children's happiness and hope for the future.

Our children are not our own—they are a gift from God. If we feel we own our kids, then it's easy to treat them as we feel like treating them, and sometimes those feelings aren't too good! If we think we own our children, then we tend to make most of their decisions and we carry the responsibility for their behavior. Then when they choose to become independent, we feel a devastating sense of loss.

If at their eighteenth birthday they're pretty good kids, then we feel an inflated sense of pride. We did it! But if they've rebelled and made some pretty lousy choices, then we suffer tremendous guilt.

I think that a much more healthy view of child rearing is that our children are a gift to us from God. He retains ownership and ultimate responsibility for them throughout their lives. We, then, are responsible to God for the way we treat His children. We shouldn't abuse them in any way or treat them as we feel like treating them. Instead, we should treat them as God Himself would treat them. And the only way we'll know how God would treat His children who are growing up in our homes is to keep the channels of communication open between us and their Owner.

Sure, we'll make mistakes, but He promises to fill in where we fail. It's amazing! God gives us His children even though He knows we're not perfect. But He expects us to do the best we can and to keep learning how to improve our parenting skills so we can continue to meet the needs of His children at each stage of their development.

Because God has created our children with the power of choice, He knows that some will go astray. But if we have done our best and asked forgiveness for our mistakes, that's all God asks of us. He doesn't want us burdened down with guilt. He has ways and means of reaching those children, if we will just release them to Him and trust Him.

If you view your children as a gift from God, then when they become independent you won't feel a bitter sense of loss. You'll feel that sense of honor for being chosen to perform this important work of using your creative talents in raising a child for God. I hope today that you feel greatly honored and will be blessed with children who will be a blessing to you and to others. That is the goal of easy obedience.

The Measure of Success

It isn't the size of your pile in the bank,
Nor the number of acres you own.
It isn't a question of prestige or rank;
Nor of sinew and muscle and bone.

It isn't the servants that come at your call,
It isn't the things you possess—
Whether many or little or nothing at all;
It's your children that measures success.

If they're happy, hardworking, honest, and kind,
Regardless of what they possess,
All the sweat and the tears spent rearing a child,
Is worth it—and measures success.

—Author Unknown